INVENTORY OF INFORMATION RESOURCES IN THE SOCIAL SCIENCES
INVENTAIRE DES SOURCES D'INFORMATION DANS LES SCIENCES
   SOCIALES

Inventaire des Sources d'Information dans les Sciences Sociales

Préparé par l'Université de Bath
pour l'Organisation de Cooperation
et de Développement Économiques

Édité par
J. M. BRITTAIN
et
S. A. ROBERTS

Inventory of Information Resources in the Social Sciences

Prepared by the University of Bath
for the Organisation for Economic
Co-operation and Development

Edited by
J. M. BRITTAIN
and
S. A. ROBERTS

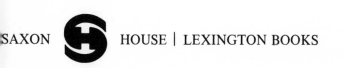

SAXON HOUSE | LEXINGTON BOOKS

Published by
SAXON HOUSE, D. C. Heath Ltd.
Westmead, Farnborough, Hants., England.

Jointly with
LEXINGTON BOOKS, D. C. Heath & Co.
Lexington, Mass. USA.

ISBN 0 347 01092 X

Printed in Great Britain
by Unwin Brothers Limited
The Gresham Press, Old Woking, Surrey
A member of the Staples Printing Group

Contents/Table des Matières

viii

Background

This inventory has been produced by the University of Bath for the Organisation for Economic Co-operation and Development.

Work began in December 1970 and drew upon work undertaken in 1969 by the OECD. Rapporteurs in each country were responsible for collecting entries within that country and for selecting their material, with the aid of a 'Guide for Rapporteurs'. During 1973 additional data were collected and an editorial revision was carried out.

Much of the editing was undertaken by Stephen Roberts and Joyce Line. Assistance was also given by Janet Ford and Ruth Sinclair, of Loughborough University, and David Nicholas, of the Polytechnic of North London. The Inventory was compiled under the direction of J. Michael Brittain, of the University of Bath.

Historique

Cet inventaire a été réalisé par l'Université de Bath à la demande de l'Organisation de Coopération et de Développement Économiques.

Le travail qui se fondait sur les travaux effectués par l'OCDE en 1969 a commencé en 1970. Des rapporteurs nationaux ont été chargés de rassembler les renseignements dans leurs pays respectifs. Un «Guide à l'intention des Rapporteurs» avait été élaboré pour leur faciliter la tâche de sélection des informations à rassembler. En 1973, des données supplémentaires ont été rassemblées qui ont entraîné une révision.

Une grande partie du travail rédactionnel a été effectué par Stephen Roberts et Joyce Line. Janet Ford et Ruth Sinclair, de l'Université de Loughborough, et David Nicholas, du «Polytechnic of North London» ont également apporté leur concours. L'inventaire a été préparé sous la direction de J. Michael Brittain, de l'Université de Bath.

Introduction

The *Inventory* provides a means of identifying, for many countries, the bodies and organisations that offer information services for social scientists.

Although most of the major social sciences have been fairly well served during the past few decades by conventional library services and bibliographical tools (for example, indexes and abstracting services), mechanised information services and data analysis centres have appeared only relatively recently. These developments have not been particularly well documented and the *Inventory* will fill this gap.

The *Inventory* should be of use to social scientists themselves, to those who supply them with information services, and to policy makers at all levels, who are concerned with the development of the social sciences and with the application, in all areas, of the results of social science research. It should also be of use to information system designers and planners, especially at an international and governmental level, where some idea of the existing state of affairs in social science information is required before decisions can be taken about future developments. Information systems in the social sciences are in need of development. Obviously the needs of social scientists themselves should be met, but it is also important that new developments be consistent with those in science information systems, to facilitate the transfer of information from one discipline to another and present users with as few difficulties of access as possible.

In addition, the development of social science information systems should be closely linked with the increasing demand for social science information stemming from users outside the social sciences. There is a growing realisation that the social sciences play an important part in the study of the relationship of science and technology to society, particularly as regards environmental problems, management in industry, the process of information transfer, and numerous other essential questions concerning modern society. But, in any case, it is now imperative to accelerate the establishment of international co-operation in the transfer and handling of social science information and to make these processes compatible with those in science. Information policy should therefore be viewed as an inseparable part of the wider policy for science, technology, and the social sciences.

Types of Information Services

The information services listed cover a wide range of activities and formats. Information services, information source publications and information research activities were originally given specific definitions[1] to meet the needs of the rapporteurs responsible for collecting data.

In the light of the experience obtained in compiling a pilot version of the *Inventory*[2] some revised operational definitions were produced. To some extent information service organisations, source publications and research activities are all generically 'information services', while differing greatly as regards such aspects as type, structure, level of organisation, accessibility, costs, formality or informality, and scope and nature of information handled. An overlapping of functions between the three types is not uncommon; query and referral activities are often linked with publication programmes of bibliographic and/or research materials and results. The revised definitions cover the three areas originally identified — information services, published information sources, and research into social science information.

Information services

The information services recorded are those organisations or activities, existing independently or within some other organisation, whose integral function and distinguishing feature is the management of information on given topics and the supply of that information to those who need or request it.

Service activities are characterised by the maintenance of files of information in various formats, and by their organisation and exploitation. Additionally, the service is often characterised by the depth and the specialised nature of the information available, the type of individual attention given to users, and the expertise shown in referring requests to other sources of information in the fields considered. The manner of carrying out the service may be bibliographical or non-bibliographical.

The information service can be developed specifically for that purpose or can exist within a library or documentation unit; its environment and external characteristics are not as important as the fact that user requests will receive specialised and individual attention, the service assuming a certain level of responsibility for meeting the users' needs.

The information collected, for each organisation providing a service, is as follows:

(a) Organisation: the name of the body responsible for providing the service. Names are given in the original language and translated into English where appropriate.

(b) Address: the postal address of the organisation and/or the information service.

(c) Title of service: the particular identifying name of the information service. It will be found that many services have no special name and are referred to by the name of the organisation.

(d) Fields covered: subject areas dealt with by the service.

(e) Availability: the type of access permitted by the information service. Three main types are recognised: (i) restricted access; (ii) access to authorised public users; and (iii) general availability.

(f) Languages: the main language associated with the service; the language range of materials covered; and the staff's linguistic capability.

(g) Charges: charges levied for facilities offered.

(h) Size, and size and type of files: usually a brief statement of the volume of bibliographical material available, the type of material available, and the number of documentation and information staff.

(i) Current system: technical systems available; usually classed as manual, mechanised, or computer-based.

Information sources

The information sources are reference or bibliographical publications providing details of the types of information potentially available to social science information users. The sources listed are mainly guides to the location, characteristics, distribution and availability of information resources (either services, other publications, or research projects) in the social sciences. The publications are available to users often as a preliminary to further contacts with information resources.

Each entry carries information corresponding to the following categories:

(a) Title of publication;
(b) Publishing organisation;
(c) Address;
(d) Fields covered;
(e) Type of information;
(f) Availability;
(g) Language(s);
(h) Frequency of publication;
(i) Price;
(j) Size;
(k) Current system.

The sources cited are a selection from the total number available, with the emphasis on those that give information about other information resources.

Information research

The section on information research contains details of research projects dealing with information activities in the social sciences. Entries give the following information:

(a) Title of project: an indicative title;
(b) Brief description: summary of the project's objectives;
(c) Names of researchers;
(d) Organisation: the organisation responsible for carrying out the project;
(e) Address;
(f) Duration of project;
(g) Source and scale of finance;
(h) Research methodology;
(i) Publications stemming from the project;
(j) Language(s).

Subjects covered, arrangement and classification of entries

The subject areas covered, all of them related either directly or indirectly to OECD concerns, are as follows: anthropology, criminology, demography, economics, education, environmental planning, ergonomics, futurology, geography, history, linguistics, management, political science, psychology, social and behavioural sciences, social policy and social administration, sociology and statistics.

Activities that concern several areas have either been classed as 'social and behavioural science', or appear under the subject category most closely related to the main area of operation. Activities specialising in one particular area of a discipline are placed within the appropriate general class. In the subject index some additional headings have been used and entries indexed under more than one heading where this seemed appropriate. Within each subject grouping, entries are arranged by country.

A number of tables summarising various aspects of coverage are reproduced in Appendix C.

Data Collection

There were two main stages in data collection. First, a pilot version was prepared using data collected by national rapporteurs in OECD member countries. The pilot version was then reviewed and an analysis indicated that coverage could be extended. The object of the second data collection, leading up to the present version of the *Inventory* was to increase coverage. Directories and bibliographies were searched and sources of information that seemed likely to qualify for an entry were contacted by letter and asked for information about relevant activities. The response was varied, but a good deal of new material was collected.

Previous Work

Although social science information services have not been entirely neglected in the past by documentalists, much of the information relating to these activities has remained scattered and has proved difficult for social scientists to obtain.

During the preparation of the *Inventory,* some familiarity with previous work and sources was required in order to establish a pattern of coverage and to supplement the data collected in the field surveys. After the pilot survey, various sources provided addresses for making further contacts with what appeared to be relevant organisations. In this respect, the *World Index of Social Science Institutions,* published by UNESCO, was valuable; but, though it indicated documentation and information services, it gave no substantive information about them.

A number of standard source directories are mentioned in Appendix B and arranged by country. Some were found useful in the preparation of the *Inventory.*

Presentation of Material

The material presented in the *Inventory* is divided into three sections: information services, information source publications, and information research. Within each section, the entries are arranged by subject, and by country within each subject. Entries are numbered consecutively, so that reference to specific entries can be made directly from the organisation, subject, and country indexes.

The absence, in any entry, of a particular data field means that no information on it was available. However, where 'negative' information was returned (for instance, where no charges were applicable to a service) this is included.

Absence of entries for the USA

In 1971, during the early stages of the compilation of the *Inventory*, it was found that the National Referral Center within the Science and Technology Division of the Library of Congress was preparing a directory, similar to the present one, of social science information resources in the United States. In view of the similarity of the two undertakings it was thought inadvisable to duplicate the material from the United States in the present *Inventory*. Thus, for American services and institutions dealing with information on the social sciences, the reader is referred to the *Directory of Information Resources in the United States: Social Sciences* (revised edition), published by the Library of Congress, Washington, 1973.

Notes

[1] See Appendix A.

[2] This was prepared during 1970 and 1971 and formed the basis of the present *Inventory*. Altogether, 19 countries were approached, and of these 14 replied. Replies were also received from a number of international bodies. The type and extent of material submitted varied greatly from one country to another; this may reflect the different information services and sources available, or it may be due to different interpretations of the 'Guide'. Rapporteurs were responsible for deciding the relevance of each information service and source, and also the amount of descriptive data reported about each resource. They were also asked to include items about which they were in doubt. After the first response, several rapporteurs were requested to supply additional data, and in some cases to check on accuracy. Further additional data were collected and checks on accuracy were made by Bath University staff, using bibliographical sources. Despite the time lag between data collection and publication, entries have been kept up-to-date wherever possible.

Introduction

L'*Inventaire* veut être un moyen d'identifier les organismes et organisations qui, dans bon nombre de pays, offrent des services d'information aux spécialistes en sciences sociales.

Durant ces dernières décennies, les services bibliothécaires et bibliographiques traditionnels (tels que répertoires, sommaires) correspondaient bien aux besoins en ce qui concerne les sciences sociales; toutefois, l'apparition, dans ces disciplines, des services d'information automatisés et des centres spécialisés dans l'analyse des données, est relativement récente. Ces nouvelles formes de services sont assez mal connues et l'Inventaire comblera cette lacune.

L'*Inventaire* devrait être utile aux spécialistes en sciences sociales eux-mêmes, à ceux qui leur fournissent des services d'information, et à tous les responsables, de quelque niveau que ce soit, qui ont affaire au développement des sciences sociales et aux multiples applications des résultats de la recherche relevant de cette discipline. Il devrait également être utile à ceux qui conçoivent et préparent les systèmes d'information, en particulier au niveau international et gouvernemental, où il est indispensable d'avoir une idée de la situation présente en matière d'information en sciences sociales avant de pouvoir prendre des décisions concernant les perfectionnements futurs. Les systèmes d'information dans le domaine des sciences sociales doivent être améliorés. Ce faisant, il convient évidemment de satisfaire aux besoins propres des spécialistes en sciences sociales, mais il importe aussi d'harmoniser l'évolution de ces systèmes avec celle des systèmes d'information relatifs aux sciences exactes et naturelles, de façon que le transfert d'information soit possible d'une discipline à l'autre et que les utilisateurs rencontrent le moins possible de difficultés d'accès.

En plus, le développement des systèmes d'information en sciences sociales devrait être étroitement lié à celui de la demande croissante d'information en sciences sociales émanant d'utilisateurs qui n'appartiennent pas à ces disciplines. De plus en plus, on se rend compte du rôle important que jouent les sciences sociales dans l'étude des relations qui existent entre, d'une part, la science et la technologie et, d'autre part, la société, les problèmes de l'environnement, la gestion industrielle, le processus des échanges d'information et bon nombre d'autres problèmes essentiels concernant la société moderne. En tous cas, il est essentiel aujourd'hui d'accélérer la mise en place d'une coopération internationale pour le transfert et le traitement de l'information en sciences sociales et de rendre ces opérations compatibles avec les processus correspondants dans le domaine scientifique. La politique de l'information devrait être considérée comme partie intégrante des politiques de la science, de la technologie et des sciences sociales.

Types de services d'information

Les services d'information répertoriés couvrent un large éventail d'activités présentant une grande diversité de formes. Les services d'information, les publications constituant des sources d'information et les travaux de recherche en matière d'information ont, à l'origine, été définis de façon précise[1] pour aider les rapporteurs chargés de rassembler les données.

A la lumière des enseignements tirés de l'élaboration de la version-pilote,[2] quelques définitions de procédure ont été révisées. Les organisations offrant un service d'information les publications relatives aux sources d'information et les travaux de recherche représentent tous, dans une certaine mesure, une variété de services d'information, bien qu'ils soient extrêmement différents sur plusieurs points: type, structure, niveau d'organisation, facilité d'accés, coûts, caractère plus ou moins officiel, étendue et nature de l'information traitée. Les fonctions de ces trois types de services débordent souvent les unes sur les autres; les activités de réponse aux demandes et de communication de référénces sont souvent liées à des programmes de publication de matériaux bibliographiques et/ou de matériaux et de résultats de recherche. Les définitions, dans leur forme révisée, couvrent les trois secteurs qui avaient été identifiés à l'origine— services d'information, sources d'information et travaux de recherche sur l'information en sciences sociales.

Services d'information

Les services d'information retenus sont les organisations ou les activités, autonomes ou rattachées à quelque autre organisation, qui ont pour fonction constitutive et distinctive de gérér l'information portant sur des sujets donnés et de la mettre à la disposition de ceux qui en ont besoin ou qui la demandent.

Les activités des services sont caractérisées par l'entretien des fichiers d'information dans leurs diverses présentations, par leur organisation et leur exploitation. En outre, le service se caractérise fréquemment par la précision et la spécificité de l'information disponible, par l'attention particulière accordée aux utilisateurs, et par la capacité à aiguiller les demandes vers d'autres formes de connaissance dans le domaine considéré. Le travail de ce service peut être de nature bibliographique ou non.

Le service d'information peut être créé exclusivement à cet effet, ou se trouver rattaché à une bibliothèque ou à une unité de documentation; son environnement et ses caractéristiques extérieures importent moins que son aptitude à répondre avec compétence aux besoins particuliers des demandeurs, et à faire preuve pour cela d'initiative.

Les renseignements rassemblés sur chaque organisation qui offre un service sont les suivants:

(a) Organisation: nom de l'organisme responsable de fournir le service. Les noms figurent dans la langue originale et sont traduits en anglais lorsque cela est nécessaire.

(b) Adresse: l'adresse postale de l'organisation et/ou du service d'information.

(c) Titre du service: le nom particulier identifiant le service. On remarquera que beaucoup de services n'ont pas de nom spécial et sont mentionnés sous celui de leur organisation.

(d) Domaines couverts: sujets couverts par le service.

(e) Disponibilité: clientèle acceptée par le service d'information. On distingue trois types différents: (i) accès réservé; (ii) accès réservé aux seuls utilisateurs extérieurs autorisés; (iii) accès à tous.

(f) Langues: langue principale en usage dans le service, langues utilisées dans les documents rassemblés, aptitudes linguistiques du personnel.

(g) Tarifs: prix demandé pour les services offerts.

(h) Taille ou taille et genre de la documentation: en général un bref résumé de l'importance de la bibliographie disponible; le genre de documentation disponible et la quantité de personnel de documentation et d'information.

(i) Système actuel: techniques du système employé qui sont rangées d'ordinaire en manuel, mécanisé, automatisé.

Les sources d'information

Les sources d'information sont des ouvrages de référence ou des bibliographies qui apportent des précisions sur les types d'information dont peuvent éventuellement disposer les utilisateurs de l'information en sciences sociales. Les sources énumérées sont pour la plupart des répertoires indiquant l'emplacement, les caractéristiques, la répartition et l'accessibilité des ressources en information (services, autres publications ou projets de recherche) dans le domaine des sciences sociales. Ces ouvrages sont souvent là pour amener les utilisateurs à d'autres contacts avec les sources d'information.

Chaque fiche comportera les rubriques suivantes:

(a) Titre de la publication;
(b) Organisation publiant la documentation;
(c) Adresse;
(d) Domaines couverts;
(e) Type d'information;
(f) Diffusion;
(g) Langue(s);
(h) Périodicité;
(i) Prix;
(j) Importance;
(k) Système actuel.

On a fait un choix parmi l'ensemble des sources en soulignant celles qui sont sources de renseignements sur d'autres sources d'information.

Recherche en matière d'information

La section consacrée à la recherche en matière d'information contient des précisions sur les projets de recherche qui traitent des activités d'information poursuivies dans le domaine des sciences sociales.

(a) Titre du projet: titre indicatif;
(b) Description succinte: résumé des objectifs du projet;
(c) Nom des chercheurs;
(d) Organisation: l'organisation responsable du projet;
(e) Adresse;
(f) Durée du projet;
(g) Source et importance du financement;
(h) Méthodes de recherche;
(i) Publications;
(j) Langue(s).

Sujets couverts, mise en ordre et classification des données

Les sujets couverts, qui se rattachent tous, directement ou indirectement, à des préoccupations de l'OCDE, sont les suivants: anthropologie, criminologie, démographie, économie, éducation, planification de l'environnement, ergonomie, futurologie, géographie, histoire, linguistique, management, sciences politiques, psychologie, sciences sociales et sciences du comportement, politique sociale et administration sociale, sociologie et statistiques.

Les activités qui empiètent sur plusieurs domaines à la fois ont été classées, soit sous la rubrique «sciences sociales et du comportement», soit dans la catégorie de sujet qui se rapprochait le plus du thème principal des travaux. Les activités qui sont spécialisées dans un domaine particulier d'une discipline donnée se trouvent sous la rubrique générale correspondante. Dans l'index par sujet, on a utilisé quelques titres supplémentaires et on a répertorié les fiches sous plusieurs rubriques lorsque cela s'avérait nécessaire. Dans le corps de l'*Inventaire*, à l'intérieur de chaque groupe de sujets, les articles sont classés par pays.

Plusieurs tableaux, récapitulant sous divers aspects les domaines couverts par l'*Inventaire,* figurent à l'Annexe C.

Collecte des données

La collecte des données s'est faite en deux grandes étapes. Tout d'abord, une version-pilote a été etablie à partir des données rassemblées dans les pays membres de l'OCDE par les rapporteurs nationaux. Cette version-pilote a été revue, et une analyse a montré que le champ couvert pouvait être élargi. Tel a donc été l'objet de la deuxième étape du travail qui a abouti a la version actuelle. Des répertoires et des bibliographies ont été méthodiquement consultés, et les organismes susceptibles de figurer dans l'*Inventaire* ont reçu des lettres leur demandant de fournir des renseignements sur les activités étudiées. Une assez grande quantité de nouveaux matériaux a ainsi été recueillie.

Travaux antérieurs

Certes, les documentalistes n'ont pas, dans le passé, totalement négligé les services d'information en sciences sociales, mais une grande partie de l'information relative à ces activités est demeurée dispersée et difficile d'accès pour les spécialistes.

Pendant la préparation de l'*Inventaire*, il s'est avéré nécessaire de se familiariser avec les travaux antérieurs et les sources existantes de façon à déterminer le champ à couvrir et à compléter les données rassemblées sur place. Une fois l'enquête-pilote terminée, diverses sources ont fourni des adresses qui ont permis d'établir d'autres contacts avec des organisations qui se sont révélées correspondre à l'objet de l'enquête. A cet égard, l'*Index mondial des institutions de sciences sociales,* publié par l'UNESCO, a été fort utile: il indique les services de documentation et d'information, sans toutefois donner de renseignements détaillés à leur sujet.

Plusieurs répertoires des sources courantes d'informations classés par pays, figurent à l'Annexe B. Certains ont servi utilement à la préparation de cet *Inventaire.*

Preséntation du matériel

Le matériel présenté dans cet *Inventaire* est réparti en trois sections: services d'information, publications relatives aux sources d'information et recherche en matière d'information.

A l'intérieur de chaque section, les articles sont classés par sujets, puis par pays à l'intérieur de chaque sujet. Ils sont numérotés consécutivement, de façon qu'il soit possible de s'y rapporter à partir des trois index, par organisations, par sujets et par pays.

Si aucun article d'inventaire ne figure dans une rubrique quelconque, c'est que l'on ne disposait d'aucune information à ce sujet. Toutefois, il est fait mention des réponses «négatives» lorsque, par exemple, aucun paiement n'est demandé par un service d'information.

Absence de matériel concernant les États-Unis

En 1971, au tout premier stade de l'élaboration de l'*Inventaire,* on a appris que le National Referral Center (Centre national de référence), rattaché à la Division de la science et de la technologie de la Bibliothèque du Congrès, États-Unis, préparait un recueil analogue à celui-ci, sur les sources d'information dans le domaine des sciences sociales aux États-Unis. Étant donnée la similitude de ces deux projets il a été jugé inopportun de reproduire dans le présent *Inventaire* le matériel concernant les États-Unis. Ainsi, pour tout renseignement concernant les services d'information et les institutions qui, en Amérique, traitent de l'information dans le domaine des sciences sociales, le lecteur est renvoyé au *Directory of Information Resources in the United States: Social Sciences* (Répertoire des ressources d'information aux États-Unis: sciences sociales), édition révisée, publié par la Bibliothèque du Congrès, Washington, 1973.

Notes

[1] Voir Annexe A.

[2] La version-pilote de l'*Inventaire,* établie au cours des années 1970 et 1971, a servi de base à la version actuelle. Dix-neuf pays en tout ont été interrogés, et quinze d'entre eux ont répondu, de même que plusieurs organismes internationaux. Le genre et l'étendue des renseignements fournis ont varié considérablement d'un pays à l'autre, ceci pouvant tenir soit aux différences relatives aux services et sources d'information disponibles, soit aux différences d'interprétation du *Guide.* Dans chaque cas les rapporteurs devaient décider s'il fallait inclure tel service ou telle source d'information et, également, déterminer la quantité de données descriptives à indiquer pour chaque ressource. Ils avaient pour instruction, en cas de doute, de consigner cependant la donnée litigieuse. Une fois la première réponse reçue, plusieurs rapporteurs ont été priés de fournir des données supplémentaires et, dans certains cas, de faire des vérifications. A partir de sources bibliographiques, l'équipe de l'Université de Bath a aussi rassemblé d'autres données supplémentaires et effectué des vérifications. Malgré le lapsé de temps qui s'est ecoulé entre la collecte des données et leur publication, les entrées ont été mises à jour dans la mesure du possible.

Abbreviations/Abréviations

Abbreviations and acronyms of titles of services, sources and research projects are given in full in the general index.

Abréviations et acronymes des titres de services, d'ouvrages de référence et des projets de recherche sont données intégralement dans l'index général.

SDI   Selective Dissemination of Information
Distribution sélectionnée d'informations

UDC Universal Decimal Classification
Classification décimale universelle

Information Services/
Services d'Information

Anthropology/Anthropologie

France

1 ORGANISATION: Centre d'Études pré- et protohistoriques
 ADDRESS: 54 rue de Varenne, Paris 7^e
 TITLE OF SERVICE: Service de Documentation
 FIELDS COVERED: Sources of energy utilised by man; progressive
   elimination of man as motive power
 TYPE OF SERVICE: Information service; consultation on the spot
 AVAILABILITY: General
 SIZE, AND TYPE OF FILES: 3,270 works. 17 periodicals.
   Photograph library
 CURRENT SYSTEM: Manual

2 ORGANISATION: École des hautes Études en Sciences sociales
 ADDRESS: 293 avenue Daumesnil, Paris 12^e
 TITLE OF SERVICE: Centre documentaire pour l'Océanie
 FIELDS COVERED: Fundamental, traditional structures; stylistic
   characteristics of Oceanic art; ethnobotany; archaeology (New
 Hebrides, Australia, Polynesia)
 TYPE OF SERVICE: Consultation on the spot; bibliographies on
   demand
 AVAILABILITY: General
 SIZE, AND TYPE OF FILES: 1,500 works. 35 periodicals
 CURRENT SYSTEM: Manual

3 ORGANISATION: École des hautes Études en Sciences sociales
 ADDRESS: 131 boulevard Saint-Michel, Paris 5^e
 TITLE OF SERVICE: Centre de Documentation sur l'Extrême-
   Orient (Section Chine)
 FIELDS COVERED: Political, economic, cultural and religious life of
   China, past and present
 TYPE OF SERVICE: Consultation on the spot; bibliographies on
   demand

3

AVAILABILITY: General
LANGUAGE(S): Language of origin
SIZE, AND TYPE OF FILES: 8,000 works, 75 periodicals, 105 rolls
   of microfilm
CURRENT SYSTEM: Manual

4   ORGANISATION: École des hautes Études en Sciences sociales
     ADDRESS: 20 rue de la Baume, Paris 8^e
     TITLE OF SERVICE: Centre d'Études africaines – (CARDAN)
     FIELDS COVERED: Economic, social and behavioural aspects of
        Black Africa (south of the Sahara) and Madagascar from
        prehistoric times to the present day
     TYPE OF SERVICE: Consultation on the spot (Centre d'Études
        africaines); bibliographies on demand
     AVAILABILITY: General
     CHARGES: Free
     SIZE, AND TYPE OF FILES: 3,500 works; 200 periodicals, of which
        20–30 are current bibliographies
     CURRENT SYSTEM: Manual

5   ORGANISATION: Laboratoire d'Anthropologie sociale
     ADDRESS: 11 place Marcelin Berthelot, Paris 5^e
     TITLE OF SERVICE: Centre documentaire d'Ethnologie comparée
     FIELDS COVERED: Life and culture of primitive peoples all over the
        world (systems of kinship, mythical representations, etc.)
     TYPE OF SERVICE: Organisation of dossiers of cultural materials.
        Consultation on the spot, information on demand
     AVAILABILITY: General
     LANGUAGE(S): Original language with English translation
     CHARGES: Free
     SIZE, AND TYPE OF FILES: 3,679 sources (in 1964)
     CURRENT SYSTEM: Human area files (Yale University) – entire
        reproduction of the sources on paper

6   ORGANISATION: Laboratoire d'Ethnologie des Hommes actuels et
        fossiles
     ADDRESS: Palais de Chaillot, Place du Trocadéro, Paris 16^e

4

TITLE OF SERVICE: Service de Documentation
FIELDS COVERED: Material cultures; development and progress of techniques; anthropo-sociology throughout the world; ethnography
TYPE OF SERVICE: Consultation on the spot. Bibliographies on demand
AVAILABILITY: General
SIZE, AND TYPE OF FILES: 200,000 works; collection of 1,100 periodicals, 300,000 photographs, 90 films, 2,500 maps, 18,000 records
CURRENT SYSTEM: Manual

7   ORGANISATION: Musée des Arts et Traditions populaires (ATP)
ADDRESS: Route de Madrid à la Porte Maillot, Paris 16^e
TITLE OF SERVICE: Service de Documentation
FIELDS COVERED: French popular arts; rural life; costumes and beliefs; festivals and dances; literature; music
TYPE OF SERVICE: (1) Consultation on the spot: scientific and documentary archives (MSS., dactylographic studies); printed documents; pictorial collection; record library; collection of objects. (2) Documentary research on demand
AVAILABILITY: General
SIZE, AND TYPE OF FILES: 4,500 MSS., 15,480 monographs, 42,210 printed works, 380 current periodicals, 25,000 sound items
CURRENT SYSTEM: Manual; automation being investigated

Criminology/Criminologie

Belgium/Belgique

8   ORGANISATION: CREDOC — Centre de Documentation juridique
ADDRESS: Rue de la Montagne 34, 1000 Bruxelles
FIELDS COVERED: Research in the field of law
TYPE OF SERVICE: Query answering; bibliographical research;
    publishing programme; dissemination of information; translation
AVAILABILITY: Restricted, mainly to jurists
LANGUAGE(S): French, Flemish
CHARGES: For photocopying, translations, and for bibliographical
    work in certain cases
SIZE, AND TYPE OF FILES: Machine-readable data; data base of
    72,000 items. 12 staff
CURRENT SYSTEM: Manual and computer-based

9   ORGANISATION: Centre d'Étude de la Délinquance juvénile (CEDJ)
ADDRESS: Avenue Jeanne 44, 1050 Bruxelles
FIELDS COVERED: Sociology, psychology, law, social psychology,
    statistics
TYPE OF SERVICE: Inquiries; reference work; bibliographical
    research
AVAILABILITY: General
LANGUAGE(S): French, Flemish
CHARGES: Photocopying
SIZE, AND TYPE OF FILES: Catalogues. One member of staff
CURRENT SYSTEM: Manual

10   ORGANISATION: Centre d'Études de Criminologie et de Médécine
    légale
ADDRESS: Parklaan 2, 2700 St. Niklaas-Waas
FIELDS COVERED: Criminology, legal medicine, psychiatry
TYPE OF SERVICE: Information service (supply of photocopies,
    bibliographical searches etc.). Publications (*Bulletin d'information*
    containing list of acquisitions. Specialist bibliographies)

AVAILABILITY: General
LANGUAGE(S): Flemish and French

France

11 ORGANISATION: Ministère de l'Intérieur
ADDRESS: 28 avenue de Friedland, Paris 8^e
TITLE OF SERVICE: Société internationale de Criminologie
FIELDS COVERED: Law and penal procedure; science of punishment; special criminology; social sciences; comparative criminology
TYPE OF SERVICE: Consultation on the spot; bibliography on demand
AVAILABILITY: General
SIZE, AND TYPE OF FILES: 2,500 works, 500 periodicals

12 ORGANISATION: Ministère de la Justice. Direction des Affaires criminelles
ADDRESS: 13 place Vendôme, Paris 1^e
TITLE OF SERVICE: Service d'Etudes pénales et de Criminologie
FIELDS COVERED: Penal sciences; criminology; relevant behavioural sciences (psychology, social psychology, sociology)
TYPE OF SERVICE: Library. Publication of research results and research in progress. The fields concerned include: the image of justice; cost of crime; the young adults; research on crime in other countries; research on the evolution of criminality. Annual publication of statistics: *Compte général de l'Administration, de la Justice criminelle, et de la Justice civile et commerciale*
AVAILABILITY: General
LANGUAGE(S): French and English
SIZE, AND TYPE OF FILES: 2,000 works, 200 dossiers, 40 periodicals
CURRENT SYSTEM: Manual

International

13   ORGANISATION: United Nations Social Defence Research Institute (UNSDRI)
ADDRESS: Via Giulia 52, 00186 Roma, Italy
TITLE OF SERVICE: Documentation and Information Services
FIELDS COVERED: Criminology and penology
TYPE OF SERVICE: Reference, referral, literature searches, bibliographies
AVAILABILITY: Mainly for the Institute's research staff; occasionally for post-graduate researchers
LANGUAGE(S): English, French, Italian
CHARGES: None
SIZE, AND TYPE OF FILES: 4,000 books, 300 periodicals, card indexes, documents. Three staff
CURRENT SYSTEM: Manual

Italy/Italie

14   ORGANISATION: Centro di giuscibernetica dell'Università di Torino
ADDRESS: Casella Postale 157, 10100 Torino
FIELDS COVERED: The centre works in the field of computer use in the legal institutions (tribunals, central and local authorities, criminology, computer-aided instruction in the legal field)
TYPE OF SERVICE: Preparation of bibliographical materials for publication. Library available to public. Publishes *Systema*
LANGUAGE(S): Italian, French and English
CHARGES: For publications
SIZE, AND TYPE OF FILES: Books and journals; files of photo-copies of articles
CURRENT SYSTEM: Manual card indexes. KWIC index on sociology of law; KWOC index in preparation on same subject

Netherlands/Pays-Bas

15   ORGANISATION: Nationaal Bureau voor Reclassering
ADDRESS: Nieuwe Schoolstraat 87, 's Gravenhage
FIELDS COVERED: Penology, criminal law, and criminology
relating to the reintegration of discharged prisoners into society
TYPE OF SERVICE: Query answering
LANGUAGE(S): Dutch
SIZE, AND TYPE OF FILES: About 500 abstracts are made each
year. About 35 journals scanned
CURRENT SYSTEM: Manual. Until 1967 the abstracts were
published. A questionnaire brought to light that users prefer to get
their information from the Bureau itself. Abstracts are grouped by
subject headings

United Kingdom/Royaume-Uni

16   ORGANISATION: British Institute of International and
Comparative Law
ADDRESS: 32 Furnival Street, London EC4
TITLE OF SERVICE: Commonwealth Legal Advisory Service
FIELDS COVERED: International and comparative law
TYPE OF SERVICE: Information
AVAILABILITY: Members

Demography/Démographie

Canada

17 ORGANISATION: University of Alberta, Department of Sociology
ADDRESS: Edmonton T69 2E1
TITLE OF SERVICE: Population Research Laboratory
FIELDS COVERED: Demographic; economic and social data relevant
to the general fields of demography and urban studies
TYPE OF SERVICE: Query answering, consultation, and contractual
research in demography and urban studies
AVAILABILITY: General
LANGUAGE: English
CHARGES: $10 per hour for programming services relating to
magnetic tape data survey; $120 per hour for computer time
(subject to revision)
SIZE, AND TYPE OF FILES: Library materials; machine-readable
data. Five staff
CURRENT SYSTEM: Machine-based — IBM 360-67 computers

United Kingdom/Royaume-Uni

18 ORGANISATION: University of Birmingham, Centre for West
African Studies
ADDRESS: PO Box 363, Birmingham, B15 2TT
TITLE OF SERVICE: Demographic Documentation Project
FIELDS COVERED: Demography and population studies in West
Africa. Development of the Birmingham collection of West
African census and demographic documents
TYPE OF SERVICE: Information and research. Development of
indexing systems; document indexing
AVAILABILITY: To workers in the subject area
LANGUAGE(S): English and French
CHARGES: None
SIZE, AND TYPE OF FILES: Dr P.K. Mitchell (Project Director) Miss
M. Madley (Research Associate). Manual card catalogues and indexe
CURRENT SYSTEM: Manual

10

19 ORGANISATION: International Planned Parenthood Federation
ADDRESS: 18–20 Lower Regent Street, London SW1Y 4PW
TITLE OF SERVICE: The information services of IPPF are in three units, all forming part of the Information, Education and Training Department.

(a) Library: covers printed materials – books, journals, pamphlets – and is responsible for their acquisition, storage and exploitation
(b) Audio-visual library: covering all forms of audio or visual aid for teaching about family planning at all levels. Includes patient leaflets, clinic posters, etc. (This service will form the nucleus of a proposed IPPF/UNESCO clearing-house for audio-visual communication materials in family planning.)
(c) Central filing system: housing files of correspondence, news clippings, annual reports from member associations, etc. (This section is shortly to become the IPPF Documentation Unit, with increased responsibilities for scanning of UN documents, etc.)

FIELDS COVERED: Family planning, population and demography, social, medical, educational and environmental aspects of human fertility
TYPE OF SERVICE: Answering of queries from all over the world (these may originate in telephone calls or correspondence, or be made in person). Referral to other sources of information where appropriate; literature searching upon demand; preparation of bibliographies and resource lists on selected topics (covering audio-visual equipment); preparation of *Library Bulletin* (acquisitions list) quarterly. Other sections of the department produce situation reports on individual countries; fact-sheets on such topics as 'falling birth rates and family planning'; *Family Planning in Five Continents* (an approximately annual review of the world family planning situation); *IPP News*, a newsletter with a circulation of 50,000–60,000 worldwide in seven languages; *IPPF Medical Bulletin* and *Research in Reproduction* (both published six times a year)
AVAILABILITY: The Library is open to anyone seriously interested in studying any aspect of human fertility or its control. Access to files is restricted; access to personnel concerned with giving advice to advisors on sex education, family planning, etc., can be arranged directly through the Visitors Advisor or via the library, in cases where studies on a particular topic can best be helped by discussion with a specialist

11

LANGUAGE(S): English is the first language of the IPPF; French and Spanish are its second languages

CHARGES: No charge for use of services. Some publications carry a charge but this is waived in all cases where this would inhibit the distribution of relevant information. Bibliographical services and publications are free of charge

SIZE, AND TYPE OF FILES: Five- by three-inch card-index catalogue for library materials; four- by six-inch card-index file for audio-visual library, with some aids filed in self-indexing sequences. No machine-readable data at present

Approximately 100 people work at IPPF Central Office in London. Of these 40-plus are involved in education and information work (15 working in 'traditional' dissemination of information). These figures include clerical support personnel. The library houses approximately 5,500 books; 15,000 pamphlets, reprints and reports; 400 current periodicals; more than 100 current newsletters; and audio-visual materials as listed in *Focus-On* publication

CURRENT SYSTEM: All systems are at present manually based

Economics/Économie

20 ORGANISATION: Banque de Bruxelles SA, Documentation
économique et financière
ADDRESS: Rue de la Régence 2, 1000 Bruxelles
FIELDS COVERED: Economics, finance
TYPE OF SERVICE: Query answering, reference work, biblio-
graphical research
AVAILABILITY: To personnel, and to members of the public with
authorisation
LANGUAGE(S): French, Flemish
CHARGES: None
SIZE, AND TYPE OF FILES: Card catalogues (approx. 275,000
entries); catalogues of periodical article references; files of
company information (approx. 50,000 entries); newspaper-cutting
files. 29 staff
CURRENT SYSTEM: Manual

21 ORGANISATION: Banque Lambert SCS
ADDRESS: Avenue Marnix 24, 1050 Bruxelles
FIELDS COVERED: Economics and finance
TYPE OF SERVICE: Bibliographical research; SDI; abstracting
AVAILABILITY: To staff and authorised students
LANGUAGE(S): French
CHARGES: For photocopying
SIZE, AND TYPE OF FILES: Card indexes. Eight staff
CURRENT SYSTEM: Manual

22 ORGANISATION: Centre de Recherches en Économie appliquée
de Bruxelles (CREAB)
ADDRESS: Avenue Woluwe Saint Lambert 72, 1200 Bruxelles
FIELDS COVERED: Data processing, management, social
psychology
TYPE OF SERVICE: Inquiries; bibliographical research

AVAILABILITY: To personnel, and to members of the public with authorisation
LANGUAGE(S): French, Flemish
CHARGES: For photocopying
SIZE, AND TYPE OF FILES: Card catalogues; periodicals. Three staff
CURRENT SYSTEM: Manual

23 ORGANISATION: Centre d'Information et de Documentation en Sciences économiques et sociales (CIDES)
ADDRESS: Rue de l'Industrie 6, 1040 Bruxelles
FIELDS COVERED: Economics and the social sciences
TYPE OF SERVICE: Query answering; inquiries; investigations; reference work; bibliographical research
AVAILABILITY: General
LANGUAGE(S): French, Flemish
SIZE, AND TYPE OF FILES: Card catalogues (approx. 1·5 million entries). Thirty-one staff
CURRENT SYSTEM: Manual and machine-based

24 ORGANISATION: Centre international de Recherches et d'Information sur l'Économie collective (CIRIEC)
ADDRESS: Quai de Rome 45, 4000 Liège
FIELDS COVERED: Collective and public economy; intervention; planning; co-operation; municipal enterprise; public enterprise
TYPE OF SERVICE: Documentation; bibliographical work
AVAILABILITY: To personnel and, in practice, to the public
LANGUAGE(S): French; some translation work in German and English
CHARGES: For photocopying
SIZE, AND TYPE OF FILES: File of abstracts, etc. Two staff
CURRENT SYSTEM: Manual

25 ORGANISATION: Comité belge de la Distribution
ADDRESS: Rue St. Bernard 60, 1060 Bruxelles
FIELDS COVERED: Distribution, marketing
TYPE OF SERVICE: Library; study service; information service (supply of photocopies, bibliographical searches, etc.); publications (*Répertoire de la Distribution belge, Terminologie de la Distribution, Guide du Marché belge, Bulletin mensuel*)
AVAILABILITY: General
LANGUAGE(S): Flemish and French

26 ORGANISATION: Institut universitaire d'Information sociale et
économique
ADDRESS: Avenue Molière 128, Bruxelles 6
FIELDS COVERED: Study of public opinion and of markets
TYPE OF SERVICE: Information service; study service; publications
(reports, information bulletin)
AVAILABILITY: Subscribers and organisations that support the
Institute receive all the publications. Searches, investigations and
the study of certain problems will also be carried out for them
LANGUAGE(S): Flemish, French
CHARGES: Subscription BFr. 7,500

27 ORGANISATION: Ministère des Affaires économiques, Direction
générale des Études et de la Documentation, Section
Documentation
ADDRESS: Rue de l'Industrie 6, 1040 Bruxelles
FIELDS COVERED: Social sciences, but mainly economics
TYPE OF SERVICE: Reference work; bibliographical research;
statistical material; press-cuttings services
AVAILABILITY: To personnel, and to members of the public with
authorisation
LANGUAGE(S): French, Flemish
CHARGES: For reprographic work
SIZE, AND TYPE OF FILES: Card catalogues. Nine staff
CURRENT SYSTEM: Manual

28 ORGANISATION: Ministère des Affaires économiques, Fonds
Quetelet, Bibliothèque centrale (Bibliothèque Fonds Quetelet)
ADDRESS: Rue de l'Industrie 6, 1040 Bruxelles
FIELDS COVERED: Statistics, economics, sociology, management
TYPE OF SERVICE: Query answering; inquiries; reference work;
bibliographical research
AVAILABILITY: General
LANGUAGE(S): French, Flemish
CHARGES: For photocopying
SIZE, AND TYPE OF FILES: Card catalogues, (approx. 1·5 million
entries), books, periodicals, machine-readable data. 30 staff
CURRENT SYSTEM: Manual and machine-based

29 ORGANISATION: Ministère des Finances, Bibliothèque centrale
ADDRESS: Rue de la Loi 14, 1000 Bruxelles

FIELDS COVERED: Law, political economy, public finance, import trade, money, statistics
TYPE OF SERVICE: Reference work; bibliographical research
AVAILABILITY: To personnel; to the public for consultation only
LANGUAGE(S): French, Flemish
CHARGES: None
SIZE, AND TYPE OF FILES: Card catalogues, periodicals (approx. 90,000 items). Six staff
CURRENT SYSTEM: Manual

30 ORGANISATION: Office belge pour l'Accroissement de la Productivité
ADDRESS: Rue de la Concorde 60, 1050 Bruxelles
FIELDS COVERED: Industrial economics, applied social sciences
TYPE OF SERVICE: Library; publications; information service (supply of photocopies, bibliographical searches, etc.)
AVAILABILITY: General
LANGUAGE(S): Flemish, French

31 ORGANISATION: Office national de l'Emploi (ONEM)
ADDRESS: Boulevard de l'Empereur 7, 1000 Bruxelles
FIELDS COVERED: Employment, unemployment, professional training
TYPE OF SERVICE: Query answering; inquiries; reference work
AVAILABILITY: General
LANGUAGE(S): French, Flemish
CHARGES: Generally no charge made
SIZE, AND TYPE OF FILES: Card catalogues (approx. 15,000 entries), periodicals. Six staff
CURRENT SYSTEM: Manual

32 ORGANISATION: Office national du Ducroire (OND)
ADDRESS: Square de Meeûs 40, 1040 Bruxelles
FIELDS COVERED: Foreign commerce insurance, insurance of Belgian investments and interests abroad, insurance of credit risks
TYPE OF SERVICE: Query answering
AVAILABILITY: General
LANGUAGE(S): French, Flemish
CHARGES: None
SIZE, AND TYPE OF FILES: Card catalogues; 120 periodicals; credit insurance document files. Three staff
CURRENT SYSTEM: Manual

33 ORGANISATION: Programmation de la Politique scientifique,
       Services du Premier Ministre (SPPS)
    ADDRESS: Rue de la Science 8, 1040 Bruxelles
    FIELDS COVERED: Political economy
    TYPE OF SERVICE: Inquiries; statistical and data processing
    AVAILABILITY: To personnel, and to members of the public with
       authorisation
    LANGUAGE(S): French, Flemish
    SIZE, AND TYPE OF FILES: Card catalogues (approx. 1,400 entries),
       periodicals. One member of staff
    CURRENT SYSTEM: Manual

34 ORGANISATION: Service de Documentation économique du
       Groupe EMPAIN
    ADDRESS: Avenue de l'Astronomie 23, 1030 Bruxelles
    FIELDS COVERED: Economics and finance
    TYPE OF SERVICE: Bibliographical research; analysis of press-
       cuttings
    AVAILABILITY: Restricted mainly to personnel
    LANGUAGE(S): French
    CHARGES: For photocopying
    SIZE, AND TYPE OF FILES: Card catalogues, periodicals, punched
       cards (Rapid-Tri system). About 3,000 items added every year
    CURRENT SYSTEM: Manual and mechanised

35 ORGANISATION: Société d'Études et d'Expansion (SEE)
    ADDRESS: Avenue Rogier 12, 4000 Liège
    FIELDS COVERED: Social sciences, economics, finance
    TYPE OF SERVICE: Information service; public relations; library;
       organisation of conferences, etc.
    AVAILABILITY: To members of the public with authorisation
    LANGUAGE(S): French
    CHARGES: For photocopying
    SIZE, AND TYPE OF FILES: Card catalogue, periodicals. Three staff
    CURRENT SYSTEM: Manual

36 ORGANISATION: Société nationale d'Investissement (SNI)
    ADDRESS: Boulevard du Régent 30, 1000 Bruxelles
    FIELDS COVERED: Economics, finance
    TYPE OF SERVICE: Inquiries; reference work; bibliographical
       research

AVAILABILITY: To personnel, and to members of the public with authorisation
LANGUAGE(S): French, Flemish
CHARGES: For photocopying
SIZE, AND TYPE OF FILES: Card catalogues (approx. 70,000 entries), periodicals. Nine staff
CURRENT SYSTEM: Manual

37 ORGANISATION: Union économique Benelux, Secrétariat Général (BNL – Benelux)
ADDRESS: Rue de la Régence 39, 1000 Bruxelles
FIELDS COVERED: Economic co-operation between Belgium, the Netherlands and Luxembourg
TYPE OF SERVICE: Query answering
AVAILABILITY: To personnel, and to members of the public with authorisation
LANGUAGE(S): French, Flemish
CHARGES: None
SIZE, AND TYPE OF FILES: Card catalogue. Two staff
CURRENT SYSTEM: Manual

Canada

38 ORGANISATION: Statistics Canada, General Time Series Section
ADDRESS: CANSIM User's Service, Room 3163, DBS Building, Tunney's Pasture, Ottawa
TITLE OF SERVICE: Canadian Socio-economic Information Management System (CANSIM)
FIELDS COVERED: Economics, management
TYPE OF SERVICE: Computerised national data base containing time series published for the most part by the Dominion Bureau of Statistics, and providing tapes or tables to subscribers
AVAILABILITY: To all subscribers
LANGUAGE(S): English
CHARGES: Standard tape – $150 per copy (2,500–5,000 series in the *Canadian Statistical Review*). Individual series – 15c per series per retrieval, with a minimum charge of $25
SIZE, AND TYPE OF FILES: Will include the total output of published statistics from Dominion Bureau of Statistics and some other Canadian data sources
CURRENT SYSTEM: Computerised

39 ORGANISATION: Documentation Centre of the Finnish Foreign
        Trade Association
    ADDRESS: Eteläesplanadi 18, 00130 Helsinki
    FIELDS COVERED: Market and marketing information, statistics,
        market surveys, information on foreign law
    TYPE OF SERVICE: Demand searches, bulletins, circulars
    AVAILABILITY: General
    LANGUAGE(S): Finnish, Swedish, English, German and French
    CHARGES: None for basic service
    CURRENT SYSTEM: Manual

40 ORGANISATION: Helsinki School of Economics, Library
    ADDRESS: Runeberginkatu 22–24, 00100 Helsinki
    TITLE OF SERVICE: FINDOC
    FIELDS COVERED: Economic and business sciences
    TYPE OF SERVICE: Indexing of economic articles published in
        approx. 80 Finnish journals. Titles of articles are translated into
        English. UDC arrangement. Published six times a year, available
        also on cards (75 × 125 mm). Reproduction service. Searches
        are made on demand
    AVAILABILITY: General
    LANGUAGE(S): Finnish, English
    CHARGES: Extensive searches are carried out on a fee-paying basis;
        otherwise free
    SIZE, AND TYPE OF FILES: 1,000 references a year
    CURRENT SYSTEM: Manual

41 ORGANISATION: Bureau d'Information des Communautés
européennes
ADDRESS: 61 rue des Belles Feuilles, Paris 16^e
FIELDS COVERED: European Community — trade, industry, social
welfare
TYPE OF SERVICE: Information service
AVAILABILITY: General
LANGUAGE(S): French
CHARGES: None
SIZE, AND TYPE OF FILES: 2,500 works, 1,500 documents

42 ORGANISATION: (1) Centre de Documentation de la Chambre de
Commerce et d'Industrie de Paris; (2) Comité technique des Centres
de Documentation des Chambres de Commerce et d'Industrie
ADDRESS: (1) 16 rue Chateaubriand, Paris 8e; (2) 7 rue Beaujon,
Paris 8^e
FIELDS COVERED: Economics, management, sociology,
demography
TYPE OF SERVICE: Bibliographical publications; inquiry service
LANGUAGE(S): French
CHARGES: Various
SIZE, AND TYPE OF FILES: (1) Centre de Paris — more than
500,000 references (increasing by 20,000 a year); (2) The other
centres — more than 1,650,000 different references
CURRENT SYSTEM: Systematic subject and geographical classific-
ations, index of over 7,000 key words. Index of all the industrial
and commercial enterprises of the Paris region

43 ORGANISATION: Centre de Documentation Sciences humaines du
Centre national de la Recherche scientifique
ADDRESS: 54 boulevard Raspail, Paris 6^e
TITLE OF SERVICE: *Bibliographie d'Économie*
FIELDS COVERED: Economics and related topics
TYPE OF SERVICE: Selective bibliographies; retrospective
searches on demand; services on profiles of interest
AVAILABILITY: University researchers, administrations, private
sector
LANGUAGE(S): French
CHARGES: By subscription

44 ORGANISATION: Institut national de la Statistique et des Études
économiques (INSEE)
ADDRESS: Direction générale – 29 Quai Branly, 75700 Paris
'Observatoires économiques régionaux' –

(1) OÉ du Sud-Ouest, 349 boulevard du Président Wilson,
Bordeaux
(2) OÉ du Nord, 60 boulevard de la Liberté, Lille
(3) OÉ de l'Ouest, place Victor Mangin, Nantes
(4) OÉ Méditerranéen, 10 rue Léon Paulet Mazaiguer, Marseille
(5) OÉ de Lyon, 84 rue de 1er Mars 1943, 69 Villeurbanne

TITLE OF SERVICE: The information services are located in Paris
and in the Observatoires économiques régionaux
FIELDS COVERED: All aspects of regional economic development,
quantitative and qualitative information
TYPE OF SERVICE: In Paris there are the following departments:
(1) Systèmes d'Information pour la Diffusion (information
gathering and storage); (2) Documentation (central library and
information service to personnel and the public; library bulletins
periodicals, etc., prepared); (3) Revues et Ouvrages (publications);
(4) Annuaires et Bulletins statistiques; (5) Impression et Diffusion
des Publications; (6) Relations extérieures et Analyse de la
Demande; (7) Bureau d'Information et d'Accueil (deals with
current requests for information from the public)
   The functions of the Observatoires économiques régionaux and
the services provided by them are as follows: (1) dissemination of
regional economic information and especially publications; (2)
query handling; (3) promotion and use of information; (4) study
of the need for economic information at the regional level; (5)
focus for documentation relating to the regions and departments
AVAILABILITY: General, to personnel and public
LANGUAGE(S): French
CHARGES: Reference facilities free; some charges for photocopies,
publications and specialised services
SIZE: About 500 staff (150 in Paris)
CURRENT SYSTEM: Manual and mechanised. Card indexes,
especially of periodical articles. Microfilm holdings of unpublished
information. Computer terminals at regional observatories, with a
wide range of data-handling facilities and programmes.

45 ORGANISATION: Laboratoire d'Économétrie du CNAM
ADDRESS: 292 rue St. Martin, Paris 3^e
FIELDS COVERED: Prices, industrial statistics, industrial
economics, econometrics
TYPE OF SERVICE: Information
AVAILABILITY: General
SIZE, AND TYPE OF FILES: 650 works, 20 reviews

46 ORGANISATION: Secrétariat aux Affaires étrangères chargé de la
Coopération
ADDRESS: 20 rue Monsieur, Paris 7^e
FIELDS COVERED: Economic co-operation, external aid, economic
development
TYPE OF SERVICE: Economic documentation service
AVAILABILITY: General
SIZE, AND TYPE OF FILES: 5,000 works, 274 periodicals, 600
dossiers

47 ORGANISATION: Institut d'Étude du Développement économique
et socialé, Université de Paris
ADDRESS: 58 boulevard Arago, Paris 13^e
TITLE OF SERVICE: Service de la Bibliothèque et de la
Documentation
FIELDS COVERED: Economic and social aspects of development
TYPE OF SERVICE: Teaching and research materials
AVAILABILITY: Members of the university
LANGUAGE(S): French

Germany (Federal Republic)/République fédérale d'Allemagne

48 ORGANISATION: Bibliothek des Instituts für Weltwirtschaft an
der Universität Kiel
ADDRESS: Kiel-Wik, Mecklenburger Strasse 2–4
FIELDS COVERED: Economics
TYPE OF SERVICE: SDI and question answering
AVAILABILITY: General
LANGUAGE(S): German
CHARGES: Only for SDI. Otherwise free
SIZE, AND TYPE OF FILES: 250,000 titles in the system, increas-
ing by 25,000 titles each year
CURRENT SYSTEM: Manual

49 ORGANISATION: Organisation for Economic Co-operation and
Development (OECD)
ADDRESS: 2 rue André Pascal, 75 Paris 16e, France
TITLE OF SERVICE: Automatic Documentation Section, Develop-
ment Enquiry Service, OECD Development Centre (AUTODOC)
FIELDS COVERED: Economic and social development
TYPE OF SERVICE: Computer storage, and retrieval of OECD
documents, the aim being to develop: (1) capacity to process
input from compatible systems; (2) a common retrieval language;
(3) a documentary software package that can be adapted to
various hardware systems
AVAILABILITY: General
CHARGES: None
CURRENT SYSTEM: Computerised

Italy/Italie

50 ORGANISATION: Associazione per lo sviluppo dell'industria nel
Mezzogiorno (SVIMEZ)
ADDRESS: Via di Porta Pinciana 6, 00187 Roma
FIELDS COVERED: Economic development
TYPE OF SERVICE: Publications, bibliographies, reports
AVAILABILITY: General
LANGUAGE(S): Italian
CHARGES: Annual subscription of Lire 4,000 for *Informazioni
SVIMEZ;* not fixed for other services

51 ORGANISATION: Banca d'Italia
ADDRESS: Via Nazionale, Roma
TITLE OF SERVICE: Il Servizio studi economici, Centro di
documentazione e archivio
FIELDS COVERED: Economics, public finance, money, banking
TYPE OF SERVICE: Information service, publications
AVAILABILITY: General
LANGUAGE(S): Italian

52 ORGANISATION: Cassa per il Mezzogiorno
ADDRESS: Piazzale Kennedy 2, Roma

TITLE OF SERVICE: (1) Ufficio programmi e documentazione;
(2) Ufficio stampa
FIELDS COVERED: Economic development
TYPE OF SERVICE: Information service; publishes periodicals and
monographs
LANGUAGE(S): Italian

53 ORGANISATION: Confederazione generale dell'industria Italiana
(Confindustria)
ADDRESS: Via Botteghe Oscure 46, Roma
TITLE OF SERVICE: Centro documentazione
FIELDS COVERED: Economic development, industrial organisation,
labour economics, public finance
TYPE OF SERVICE: Consultations; exchange of publications and
information
CURRENT SYSTEM: Manual; own classification

54 ORGANISATION: Istituto di economica agraria (INEA)
ADDRESS: Via Barberini 36, Roma
TITLE OF SERVICE: Ufficio annuario; Publicazioni
FIELDS COVERED: Economic and political factors in
agriculture and rural sociology
TYPE OF SERVICE: Information service, bibliographical research;
photocopying
AVAILABILITY: General
LANGUAGE(S): Italian
CHARGES: None
SIZE, AND TYPE OF FILES: 14,000 books, 400 periodicals
CURRENT SYSTEM: Manual

55 ORGANISATION: Istituto nazionale per lo studio della
congiuntura (ISCO)
ADDRESS: Via Palermo 20, Roma
TITLE OF SERVICE: Information and documentation centre
FIELDS COVERED: Economics, statistics, and research methodology
TYPE OF SERVICE: Information; preparation of bibliographical
materials
AVAILABILITY: General
LANGUAGE(S): Italian
CHARGES: None
CURRENT SYSTEM: Manual

56 ORGANISATION: Unione italiana delle camere di commercio, industria, artigianato e agricoltura
ADDRESS: Piazza Sallustio 21, Roma
TITLE OF SERVICE: Library
FIELDS COVERED: Statistics, economics, economic geography
TYPE OF SERVICE: Information and documentation
AVAILABILITY: Generally to students, researchers, statisticians, journalists
LANGUAGE(S): Italian, French, English
CHARGES: None
CURRENT SYSTEM: Manual; uses own classification scheme

57 ORGANISATION: Servizio affari generali Ministero trasporti, Direzione generale FS
ADDRESS: Piazza della Croce Rossa, 00161 Roma
TITLE OF SERVICE: Centro di documentazione
FIELDS COVERED: Rail and other transport
TYPE OF SERVICE: Bibliographies, photocopies, abstracts, translation
AVAILABILITY: General, with certain limitations
LANGUAGE(S): Italian
CHARGES: Not specified
SIZE, AND TYPE OF FILES: 40,000 books, 110 periodicals, 1,500 diverse documents
CURRENT SYSTEM: Manual; own classification

Japan/Japon

58 ORGANIZATION: Institute for Economic Research, Hitotsubashi University
ADDRESS: 185 Kunitachi, Kunitachi-shi, Tokyo
TITLE OF SERVICE: Documentation Centre for Japanese Economic Statistics
FIELDS COVERED: Japanese economic statistics
TYPE OF SERVICE: Catalogue; indexing; query answering service, SDI service
AVAILABILITY: General researcher
LANGUAGE(S): Japanese
CHARGES: None
CURRENT SYSTEM: Mechanised retrieval

25

59 ORGANISATION: Japan External Trade Organisation
ADDRESS: Aoi, Akasaka, Minato-ku, Tokyo
TITLE OF SERVICE: International Trade Information Centre
FIELDS COVERED: Trade, economics
TYPE OF SERVICE: Query answering service
AVAILABILITY: General researcher
LANGUAGE(S): Japanese
CHARGES: None
SIZE, AND TYPE OF FILES: Data accumulated for about
   300,000 cases
CURRENT SYSTEM: Computerised

60 ORGANISATION: Research Institute for Economics and Business
   Administration, Kobe University
ADDRESS: Rokkodai-machi, Nada-ku, Kobe
TITLE OF SERVICE: Documentation Centre for Business Analysis
FIELDS COVERED: Industrial administration, economics
TYPE OF SERVICE: Catalogue; indexing; query answering service,
   SDI service
AVAILABILITY: General researcher
LANGUAGE(S): Japanese
CHARGES: None

Netherlands/Pays-Bas

61 ORGANISATION: Economische Voorlichtingsdienst (EVD) van het
   Ministerie van Economische Zaken
ADDRESS: Bezuidenhoutseweg 151, 's Gravenhage.
FIELDS COVERED: Economics (theoretical, management economics
   marketing, market information)
TYPE OF SERVICE: Specialised library; question answering;
   literature surveys; SDI service
AVAILABILITY: General
LANGUAGE(S): Dutch, English, French, German
CHARGES: SDI – Hfl. 30 for bulletins; Hfl. 0·14 per fiche. Other
   services free
CURRENT SYSTEM: Computerisation in progress. Subjects grouped
   according to UDC

62 ORGANISATION: The Anglo-Japanese Economic Institute
ADDRESS: 342 Grand Buildings, Trafalgar Square, London WC2
TITLE OF SERVICE: Economic Information Unit on Japan
TYPE OF SERVICE: Information

63 ORGANISATION: Commonwealth Bureau of Agricultural
Economics
ADDRESS: 31a St. Giles, Oxford
FIELDS COVERED: Agricultural economics; rural sociology
TYPE:OF SERVICE: Information service, largely through WAERSA
(World Agricultural Economics and Rural Sociology Abstracts)

64 ORGANISATION: Confederation of British Industry
ADDRESS: 21 Tothill Street, London SW1
FIELDS COVERED: British industry, management
TYPE OF SERVICE: Librarian and information officer
LANGUAGE(S): English

65 ORGANISATION: Department of Employment and Productivity,
Training Department
ADDRESS: 168 Regent Street, London W1
TITLE OF SERVICE: Training Abstracts Service
FIELDS COVERED: Industrial training and further education
TYPE OF SERVICE: Abstracting
AVAILABILITY: On subscription
LANGUAGE(S): English
CHARGES: £5–£50
SIZE, AND TYPE OF FILES: 960 abstracts per year (all on cards);
100 specialist periodicals

66 ORGANISATION: Department of Trade
ADDRESS: (1) 1 Victoria Street, London SW1; (2) Hillgate House,
35 Old Bailey, London EC4
TITLE OF SERVICE: DOT Library Services – (1) Central Library;
(2) Statistics and Market Intelligence Library
FIELDS COVERED: Social sciences
TYPE OF SERVICE: Information and reference library
AVAILABILITY: (1) by appointment; (2) general
LANGUAGE(S): English

67 ORGANISATION: The Economist Intelligence Unit Ltd.
ADDRESS: Spencer House, 27 St. James's Place, London SW1
FIELDS COVERED: Marketing, economic and sociological research
TYPE OF SERVICE: Inquiry service
AVAILABILITY: General; library not available for reference purpose
LANGUAGE(S): English
CHARGES: On a fee-paying basis

68 ORGANISATION: The Institute of Bankers Library
ADDRESS: 10 Lombard Street, London EC3
FIELDS COVERED: Banking and finance
TYPE OF SERVICE: Library
AVAILABILITY: Primarily to Institute members
LANGUAGE(S): English

69 ORGANISATION: London and Cambridge Economic Service
ADDRESS: London School of Economics and Political Science,
    Houghton Street, Aldwych, London WC2
FIELDS COVERED: Statistical information; interpretation of
    current economic developments in UK and elsewhere
TYPE OF SERVICE: Information service
LANGUAGE(S): English

70 ORGANISATION: Royal Institution of Chartered Surveyors
ADDRESS: 12 Great George Street, London SW1
TITLE OF SERVICE: Technical Information Service
FIELDS COVERED: Planning and development; all aspects of
    property and surveying
TYPE OF SERVICE: Inquiry and publications
AVAILABILITY: Inquiry service on fee-paying basis to non-
    members, publications to members only
LANGUAGE(S): English
CHARGES: See above

71 ORGANISATION: Scott Polar Research Institute
ADDRESS: Lensfield Road, Cambridge
FIELDS COVERED: Polar regions; economic development of
    the Arctic
TYPE OF SERVICE: Information provision;
    library
LANGUAGE(S): English

28

Education/Éducation

72 ORGANISATION: Association internationale pour la Recherche et la Diffusion des Méthodes audio-visuelles et structuro-globales (AIMAV)
ADDRESS: Avenue Georges Bergmann 109, 1050 Bruxelles
TITLE OF SERVICE: Dissemination of information and research results
FIELDS COVERED: Research and popularisation activities in fields of linguistics, teaching, literature, sociology, media, technology
TYPE OF SERVICE: Research conducted at university level
LANGUAGE(S): French, Flemish, English, German, Spanish, Italian, Russian
TYPE OF FILES: Research files

73 ORGANISATION: Centre belge de Documentation musicale, ASBL (CeBeDeM)
ADDRESS: c/o Bibliothèque royale Albert Ier, Boulevard de l'Empereur 4, 1000 Bruxelles
FIELDS COVERED: Music
TYPE OF SERVICE: Information service; library; record library; music publishing; query answering; reference work; bibliographical research; location of material
AVAILABILITY: General
LANGUAGE(S): French, Flemish, English, German
CHARGES: For photocopying; otherwise none
SIZE, AND TYPE OF FILES: Catalogues, microfilms, gramophone records. Nine staff
CURRENT SYSTEM: Manual

74 ORGANISATION: Europees Studie- en Informatiecentrum
ADDRESS: Handelsbeurs, 1ste verdieping, Twaalfmaandenstraat, 2000 Antwerpen
FIELDS COVERED: Popular education around the theme of a unified Europe

TYPE OF SERVICE: Specialised library; organises study sessions; lectures; colloquia
AVAILABILITY: General
LANGUAGE(S): Flemish, French, English, German
CHARGES: None
SIZE: Three staff
CURRENT SYSTEM: Manual

75 ORGANISATION: Ministère de l'Éducation nationale et de la Culture française (Direction générale de l'Organisation des Études) Bibliothèque centrale
ADDRESS: Rue de Louvain 27, 1000 Bruxelles
FIELDS COVERED: Education; all aspects of teaching
TYPE OF SERVICE: Prepares lists of new material acquired
AVAILABILITY: To personnel, and to members of the public with authorisation
LANGUAGE(S): French
CHARGES: For photocopying
SIZE, AND TYPE OF FILES: Card catalogues. Eleven staff
CURRENT SYSTEM: Manual

76 ORGANISATION: Ministerie van nationale Opvoeding en Nederlandse Cultuur Documentatiedienst en Bibliotheek
ADDRESS: Leuvenseweg 27, 1000 Brussel
FIELDS COVERED: Education and teaching
TYPE OF SERVICE: Library; book loan service
AVAILABILITY: To personnel, and to members of the public with authorisation
LANGUAGE(S): Flemish, Dutch
CHARGES: For photocopying
SIZE, AND TYPE OF FILES: Card catalogues. Eleven staff
CURRENT SYSTEM: Manual

77   ORGANISATION: Association of Universities and Colleges of
Canada, and Canadian Society for the Study of Higher Education
ADDRESS: 151 Slater Street, Ottawa K1P 5NI, Ontario
TITLE OF SERVICE: Inventory of ongoing research projects
relevant to higher education in Canada
FIELDS COVERED: Research into higher education
TYPE OF SERVICE: File of material and reports (mostly 1970) in
the AUCC library. Material to be published in *Stoa* and *University
Affairs* (abridged details). Updating planned to take place twice a
year
AVAILABILITY: General
CHARGES: No charge; journals on subscription
SIZE: 100 projects (early 1972)
CURRENT SYSTEM: Manual

78   ORGANISATION: Ontario Institute for Studies in Education
ADDRESS: 252 Bloor St. West, Toronto 5, Ontario
TITLE OF SERVICE: Director's Office, Information Service
FIELDS COVERED: Education
TYPE OF SERVICE: Reception and referral of queries; query
answering
AVAILABILITY: General
LANGUAGE(S): English
SIZE: Three staff

79   ORGANISATION: Ontario Institute for Studies in Education
ADDRESS: 252 Bloor St. West, Toronto 5, Ontario
TITLE OF SERVICE: Information Services, Office of the
Co-ordinator of Research and Development Studies
FIELDS COVERED: Provides information only on studies conducted
by Institute staff. Such studies are related to education, psychology,
sociology of education, measurement and evaluation, and special
and remedial education. Specific subjects include: diagnosis, nature
and remediation of learning disabilities; history and philosophy of
education; educational planning; educational administration; adult
education; continuing education; post-secondary education;
application of computer technology in education; education media
(both the production and evaluation of such media); curriculum
development and evaluation; diffusion and dissemination of

31

educational curricula and/or methodology (including innovative administrative structure or practice)

TYPE OF SERVICE: Answering specific inquiries; limited preparation of bibliographical materials; providing abstracts or copies of project outlines and reports; referral services, including liaison between inquirers and investigators

AVAILABILITY: The service is available to the public generally, but is known, for the most part, only to those professionally involved in public education or to other academic institutions

LANGUAGE(S): Services are really only provided in English, but at present there are persons capable of handling inquiries in French or Spanish as well

CHARGES: There is no charge for information services. If an inquirer requests photocopies of extremely lengthy documents he is sometimes asked to pay the costs

SIZE, AND TYPE OF FILES: (1) Project files contain copies of all project proposals submitted for central funding, and progress reports or other products resulting from projects approved and funded. (2) Besides all the Institute's formal publications, the Research and Development library contains approximately 1,000 papers, working papers, progress reports, curricula, etc., produced by Institute staff. Most of this material is in print or typescript. Three part-time staff

CURRENT SYSTEM: Manual

80   ORGANISATION: Ontario Institute for Studies in Education, Library

ADDRESS: 252 Bloor St. West, Toronto 5, Ontario

FIELDS COVERED: Education, social sciences generally (e.g. sociology, psychology), humanities (e.g. history, philosophy)

TYPE OF SERVICE: Services include query answering and reference work; referral to individuals and institutions that are known to have information; literature searches; preparation of bibliographies and annotated bibliographies; indexing and abstracting

AVAILABILITY: Available to the educational public, primarily in the Province of Ontario; available to the general public through referral from individuals or institutions

LANGUAGE(S): Language of transaction, English; limited transaction in French, according to need

CHARGES: No charges for service, except for costs of photocopying and inter-library loans

SIZE, AND TYPE OF FILES: Files held: books, including periodicals and serials; microfiche and microfilm (research reports, theses, periodicals); films; other audio-visual resources (e.g. audiotapes, videotapes, etc.); instructional materials (kits, games, etc.); press-clippings; university calendars; standardised tests (historical file).

Staff engaged in information activities (excluding library staff not actively involved in reference and referral services): reference and information services — four librarians, five assisting staff; audio-visual services — one librarian, 1·5 assisting staff; instructional materials — one librarian, 1·5 assisting staff
CURRENT SYSTEM: Manual; links to computerised systems (e.g. ERIC) being considered

31 ORGANISATION: Ontario Institute for Studies in Education, Modern Language Centre
ADDRESS: 252 Bloor St. West, Toronto 5, Ontario
TITLE OF SERVICE: Information and field services
FIELDS COVERED: Modern languages; teaching of second languages
TYPE OF SERVICES:

(1)   Consultation and information: research, materials development, and language teaching programmes (staff)
(2)   Documents collection: a reference collection of documents on language theory and language teaching
(3)   Language teaching materials collection: a collection of textbooks, tapes, films, filmstrips, and other language teaching aids, available for reference in the Centre
(4)   Technological facilities including: (a) 40-position language laboratory, incorporating closed-circuit television; (b) viewing room for inspecting language learning materials; (c) recording studio fitted for broadcast-quality recording; and (d) tape library with an expanding collection of language instruction tapes.

Limited facilities for second language learning are available to the staff and students of OISE
AVAILABILITY: General
LANGUAGE(S): Various
CURRENT SYSTEM: Manual and mechanised

82 ORGANISATION: Université Laval, Centre de Documentation
ADDRESS: Université Laval, Quebec 10e, PQ
TITLE OF SERVICE: Centre de Documentation
FIELDS COVERED: Human sciences, pure and applied sciences
TYPE OF SERVICE: Interdisciplinary documentation centre for
teaching and research; keyword indexes; information retrieval;
publication programme
AVAILABILITY: Mainly to students and staff of Laval University,
but outside users may apply to receive services
SIZE, AND TYPE OF FILES: Large microfilm files; primary material
CURRENT SYSTEM: Mechanised and computer-based for internal
operations

Finland/Finlande

83 ORGANISATION: University of Jyväskylä, Library and Institute
for Educational Research
ADDRESS: 40100 Jyväskylä
TITLE OF SERVICE: ERIC (Research in education)
FIELDS COVERED: Education
TYPE OF SERVICE: SDI service. Inquiry service and publishing of

(1) annual bibliography of educational literature in Finland
(also published in Scandinavian educational bibliography);
(2) annual bibliography of educational research projects in
Finland;
(3) annual bibliography of theses in education (published in
Kasvatus, the Finnish Journal of Education)

AVAILABILITY: General
LANGUAGE(S): ERIC — English; others — Finnish. Abstracts in
English, when needed
CHARGES: ERIC — charges not yet determined; other services
generally free of charge
CURRENT SYSTEM: Manual and IBM 360

France

84 ORGANISATION: Centre de Formation et de Recherches de
l'Éducation surveillée
ADDRESS: 54 rue de Garches, Vaucresson 92
TITLE OF SERVICE: Centre de Documentation
FIELDS COVERED: Pedagogics, psycho-pedagogics, sociology of
education, criminology, juvenile delinquency
TYPE OF SERVICE: Inquiry service, bibliographies on demand.
Publishes *Bulletin bibliographique*
AVAILABILITY: General
LANGUAGE(S): French
SIZE, AND TYPE OF FILES: 15,000 works; 250 periodicals;
judicial statistics of delinquency
CURRENT SYSTEM: Manual

85 ORGANISATION: Division du développement social des Nations
Unies (FISE), Gouvernement français
ADDRESS: Château de Longchamp, Bois de Boulogne, Paris 16ᵉ
TITLE OF SERVICE: Conseil international de l'Enfance (CIE)
FIELDS COVERED: Pedagogics, applied paediatrics, training of
medical, social and teaching personnel
TYPE OF SERVICE: Bibliographical search service on subscription
and on demand; despatch of photocopies and microfilms
AVAILABILITY: General
CHARGES: Bibliographical references: inclusive subscription
Fr. 800; partial subscription Fr. 0·10 per fiche. Bibliographies:
cost of searches Fr. 40.
SIZE, AND TYPE OF FILES: 12,800 works; files containing some
2,500,000 bibliographical references

86 ORGANISATION: Éducation nationale, Institut pédagogique
national
ADDRESS: 3 rue Roquelaine, Toulouse 31
TITLE OF SERVICE: Centre régional de Documentation
pédagogique (CRDP)
FIELDS COVERED: Applied pedagogical research; new teaching
techniques. Encyclopaedic documentation
TYPE OF SERVICE: Inquiry service; lending of documents to
members of l'Éducation nationale
AVAILABILITY: General

LANGUAGE(S): French
SIZE, AND TYPE OF FILES: 18,500 works (of which about 10,000
are in the domain of pedagogics); 250 periodicals (a great
proportion of which are pedagogical reviews)
CURRENT SYSTEM: Automation of cataloguing is planned

87 ORGANISATION: Ministère des Affaires sociales, Centre technique
national pour l'Enfance et l'Adolescence inadaptées
ADDRESS: 1 rue du 11 Novembre, Montrouge 92
TITLE OF SERVICE: Centre de Documentation
FIELDS COVERED: Public health, teaching, maladjustment,
delinquency, law, social life, social action, psychology, psychiatry,
therapeutic methods
TYPE OF SERVICE: Consultation; bibliography on demand
AVAILABILITY: General
CHARGES: None
SIZE, AND TYPE OF FILES: 3,500 works, 200 periodicals
CURRENT SYSTEM: Manual

Germany (Federal Republic)/République fédérale d'Allemagne

88 ORGANISATION: Informationszentrum für Fremdsprachenforschun
ADDRESS: Marburg/Lahn, Liebigstrasse 37
TITLE OF SERVICE: *Bibliographie moderner
Fremdsprachenunterricht*
FIELDS COVERED: Language teaching methods, technology of
language instruction, psycholinguistics
TYPE OF SERVICE: Query answering
AVAILABILITY: General
LANGUAGE(S): German
CURRENT SYSTEM: Manual

89 ORGANISATION: Pädagogisches Zentrum Berlin
ADDRESS: Berlin 31, Berliner Strasse 40–41
TITLE OF SERVICE: (1) *Bibliographie Pädagogik;* (2) *Bibliographie
programmierter Unterricht*
FIELDS COVERED: Education
TYPE OF SERVICE: Query answering
AVAILABILITY: General
LANGUAGE(S): German
CURRENT SYSTEM: Computerised

90 ORGANISATION: Schulbauinstitut der Länder
ADDRESS: Berlin 12, Strasse des 17. Juni 112
TITLE OF SERVICE: *Schulbaubibliographie*
FIELDS COVERED: School architecture
TYPE OF SERVICE: Query answering
AVAILABILITY: General
LANGUAGE(S): German
SIZE, AND TYPE OF FILES: Approx. 10,000 titles
CURRENT SYSTEM: Manual

International

91 ORGANISATION: Council of Europe
ADDRESS: avenue de l'Europe, Strasbourg 67, France
TITLE OF SERVICE: Documentation Centre for Education in
Europe
FIELDS COVERED: Educational and cultural development in the
member states of the Council of Europe/Council for Cultural
Co-operation
TYPE OF SERVICE: Information service. Abstracts published
irregularly in loose-leaf form, summarising the important policy,
legislative and administrative texts bearing on education in the
member states. *Information Bulletin* published three times
annually, *Newsletter* six times annually
AVAILABILITY: General
LANGUAGE(S): English and French
CHARGES: None
SIZE, AND TYPE OF FILES: Varying
CURRENT SYSTEM: UDC (adapted)

92 ORGANISATION: Internationaal Audio-Visueel Technisch Centrum/
Centre Technique audio-visuel international (AVINTER)
ADDRESS: Lamorinierestraat 236, 2000 Antwerpen
FIELDS COVERED: Audio-visual techniques, technology, teaching
TYPE OF SERVICE: Query answering, reference work, biblio-
graphical research
AVAILABILITY: General
LANGUAGE(S): Dutch, French, English, German
CHARGES: For photocopying; varying charges for bibliographical
research

TYPE OF FILES: Card catalogues
CURRENT SYSTEM: Manual

93 ORGANISATION: Internationales Zentralinstitut für das Jugend-
und Bildungsfernsehen
ADDRESS: München 2, Rundfunkplatz 1
TITLE OF SERVICE: *Bibliographie Schulfernsehen*
FIELDS COVERED: Instructional television, screen education,
television didactics
TYPE OF SERVICE: Query answering
AVAILABILITY: General
LANGUAGE(S): German
CURRENT SYSTEM: Manual

94 ORGANISATION: UNESCO
ADDRESS: 7 rue Eugène Delacroix, Paris 16^e
TITLE OF SERVICE: Institut international de Planification de
l'Éducation
FIELDS COVERED: Teaching and economic development; foreign
aid and technical assistance; techniques of teaching
TYPE OF SERVICE: Specialised library possessing reports having a
limited distribution; inquiry service
AVAILABILITY: Access restricted to members of the Institute and
to persons provided with an introduction
SIZE, AND TYPE OF FILES: 16,000 works, 250 periodicals
CURRENT SYSTEM: Manual

Netherlands/Pays-Bas

95 ORGANISATION: Ministerie van Onderwijs en Wetenschappen,
Afd. Documentatie
ADDRESS: Nieuwe Uitleg 1, 's Gravenhage
FIELDS COVERED: Education, science policy, information policy
TYPE OF SERVICE: Query answering, bibliographies, literature
reports
AVAILABILITY: General
LANGUAGE(S): Dutch
CHARGES: None
SIZE, AND TYPE OF FILES: About 100 literature reports
a year
CURRENT SYSTEM: Manual; classification by UDC

96 ORGANISATION: Centrum voor Studie van het Onderwijs in
veranderende Maatschappijen/ Centre for the Study of Education
in Changing Societies
ADDRESS: Molenstraat 27, 's Gravenhage
FIELDS COVERED: Educational problems in developing countries,
and all related subjects
TYPE OF SERVICE: Query answering, literature searches,
preparation of bibliographical materials
AVAILABILITY: Restricted
LANGUAGE(S): English
CHARGES: Forwarding charges only
SIZE, AND TYPE OF FILES: 1,500 books; 1,100 documents; card
indexes
CURRENT SYSTEM: Manual

Sweden/Suède

97 ORGANISATION: Statens Psykologisk-Pedagogiska Bibliotek
ADDRESS: Box 23099, S104 35 Stockholm 23
TITLE OF SERVICE: ERIC (microfilms and tapes)
FIELDS COVERED: Education, psychology
TYPE OF SERVICE: Selective dissemination of information
AVAILABILITY: General
LANGUAGE(S): English, Swedish, German, French
SIZE, AND TYPE OF FILES: 140,000 volumes, 650 current
periodicals
CURRENT SYSTEM: Computer based (ERIC); library catalogues
arranged by subject (Swedish SAB system), alphabetically, and by
keyword

Switzerland/Suisse

98 ORGANISATION: Institut romand de Recherches et de
Documentation pédagogiques
ADDRESS: Fbg. Hôpital 43, Neuchâtel
FIELDS COVERED: Education and teaching to pre-university level
TYPE OF SERVICE: Information service
AVAILABILITY: Available to the Swiss teaching profession
LANGUAGE(S): French
CHARGES: None for members

99   ORGANISATION: Schweizerische Dokumentationsstelle für
     Schul- und Bildungsfragen
     ADDRESS: Palais Wilson, 52 rue des Paquis, 1211 Genève 14
     FIELDS COVERED: Teaching and education
     TYPE OF SERVICE: Information and advice
     AVAILABILITY: General
     LANGUAGE(S): French, German, English

United Kingdom/Royaume-Uni

100 ORGANISATION: Advisory Centre for Education (ACE)
     ADDRESS: 32 Trumpington Street, Cambridge
     TITLE OF SERVICE: British Education Data Bank
     FIELDS COVERED: All aspects of education
     TYPE OF SERVICE: Information and advice on education are
     available from the Advisory Service, within which the British
     Education Data Bank has recently been set up
     AVAILABILITY: To subscribers
     LANGUAGE(S): English
     CHARGES: Subscription to ACE. Short queries answered free of
     charge; longer queries requiring detailed research dealt with for a
     fee. Fees vary from 50p to £5. (Membership includes a year's
     issues of *Where*, which prints factual, up-to-date reports on all
     aspects of education)

101 ORGANISATION: Association for Programmed Learning and
     Educational Technology
     ADDRESS: 27 Torrington Square, London WC1
     FIELDS COVERED: Educational technology
     TYPE OF SERVICE: Referral to experts
     LANGUAGE(S): English

102 ORGANISATION: British Association for Commercial and
     Industrial Education
     ADDRESS: 16 Park Crescent, London W1N 4AP
     FIELDS COVERED: Vocational training, further and higher
     education
     TYPE OF SERVICE: Information service. Publishes *Register of
     Programmed Instruction*

40

AVAILABILITY: *Register* is generally available; information service for members only
LANGUAGE(S): English
SIZE, AND TYPE OF FILES: 1,000 books, 1,000 pamphlets, 400 reports, 100 current periodicals

103 ORGANISATION: The British Council
ADDRESS: 65 Davies Street, London W1Y 2AA
TITLE OF SERVICE: English Teaching Information Centre
FIELDS COVERED: Teaching of English language overseas
TYPE OF SERVICE: Library; bibliographical and other information. Joint publisher of *Language Teaching Abstracts*
AVAILABILITY: General
LANGUAGE(S): English

104 ORGANISATION: Careers Research and Advisory Centre (CRAC)
ADDRESS: Bateman Street, Cambridge
FIELDS COVERED: Education and employment
TYPE OF SERVICE: Information office
LANGUAGE(S): English

105 ORGANISATION: Centre for Information on Language Teaching (CILT)
ADDRESS: State House, 63 High Holborn, London WC1
FIELDS COVERED: Modern languages with emphasis on English as a second language; linguistics, language studies and teaching media
TYPE OF SERVICE: Inquiries; preparation of bibliographies, lists of current research
AVAILABILITY: General
LANGUAGE(S): English
CHARGES: None
SIZE, AND TYPE OF FILES: 21,100 books, 355 current periodicals, 325 filmstrips, 1,000 speech records, 1,550 tape recordings, 100 microfiches

NOTE: Libraries jointly maintained by English Teaching Information Centre, British Council, and Centre for Information on Language Teaching

106 ORGANISATION: Centre for Information on the Teaching of English
ADDRESS: Moray House College of Education, Holyrood Road, Edinburgh 8

TITLE OF SERVICE: CITE
FIELDS COVERED: Teaching of English language and literature
TYPE OF SERVICE: Information and documentation
AVAILABILITY: General
LANGUAGE(S): English

107 ORGANISATION: Commonwealth Institute
ADDRESS: Kensington High Street, London W8
FIELDS COVERED: Commonwealth
TYPE OF SERVICE: Contemporary reference library; especially
geared to educational requirements
AVAILABILITY: General
LANGUAGE(S): English

108 ORGANISATION: Council for Educational Technology (CET)
ADDRESS: 160 Great Portland Street, London W1
FIELDS COVERED: Educational technology
TYPE OF SERVICE: Referral and advice

109 ORGANISATION: Language Teaching Information Centre
ADDRESS: 31 Harrogate Road, Leeds 7
FIELDS COVERED: Linguistics, language teaching, teaching
materials
TYPE OF SERVICE: Information
AVAILABILITY: General
LANGUAGE(S): English, German, Spanish, Russian

110 ORGANISATION: National Committee for Audio-Visual Aids in
Education
ADDRESS: 33 Queen Anne Street, London W1M 0AL
FIELDS COVERED: Audio-visual matters
TYPE OF SERVICE: Information service
AVAILABILITY: General
LANGUAGE(S): English

111 ORGANISATION: National Institute of Adult Education
(England and Wales)
ADDRESS: 35 Queen Anne Street, London W1M 0BL
TITLE OF SERVICE: None
FIELDS COVERED: Adult education
TYPE OF SERVICE: Inquiry

AVAILABILITY: General
LANGUAGE(S): English
SIZE, AND TYPE OF FILES: 2,000 books and pamphlets,
  20 current periodicals

112 ORGANISATION: National Society for Autistic Children
ADDRESS: 1a Golders Green Road, London NW11
FIELDS COVERED: Autistic children
TYPE OF SERVICE: Information and advisory service
AVAILABILITY: General
LANGUAGE(S): English

113 ORGANISATION: The Royal National Institute for the Deaf
ADDRESS: 105 Gower Street, London WC1
TITLE OF SERVICE: Information service
FIELDS COVERED: Human communication and disorders in
  hearing, speech
TYPE OF SERVICE: Information service
AVAILABILITY: General
LANGUAGE(S): English
SIZE, AND TYPE OF FILES: 6,500 books, 9,000 pamphlets

114 ORGANISATION: Society for Research into Higher Education Ltd.
ADDRESS: 20 Gower Street, London WC1
FIELDS COVERED: Research into higher education
TYPE OF SERVICE: Collection and dissemination of information
LANGUAGE(S): English

115 ORGANISATION: United Kingdom National Documentation Centre
  for Sport, Physical Education and Recreation
ADDRESS: University of Birmingham, PO Box 363, Birmingham
  B15 2TT. Telephone (Sports Documentation Centre) 021-472-
  7410
FIELDS COVERED: Comprehensive and interdisciplinary aspects of
  sport, physical education, recreation and leisure
TYPE OF SERVICE: Mainly referral, supplying references to
  relevant literature. Query answering. Current awareness
  publications:

  (1) monthly selection of recent publications in the field of
  sport, leisure, physical education, recreation;

(2)   Sports information, *Monthly Bulletin*

Panel of translators
AVAILABILITY: General
LANGUAGE(S): English

116 ORGANISATION: University of Birmingham, National Centre for
Programmed Learning
ADDRESS: 50 Wellington Road, Edgbaston, Birmingham 15
FIELDS COVERED: Programmed learning
TYPE OF SERVICE: Collection and dissemination of information
AVAILABILITY: General
LANGUAGE(S): English

117 ORGANISATION: University of London, Institute of Education
ADDRESS: 11/13 Ridgmount Street, London WC1
FIELDS COVERED: Education
TYPE OF SERVICE: Specialist bibliographies prepared as
requested; inquiry service
AVAILABILITY: To members of the Institute and accredited
inquirers
LANGUAGE(S): English
SIZE, AND TYPE OF FILES: 85,000 books, 15,000 pamphlets,
1,300 periodicals

Environmental Planning/
Planification de l'Environnement

Austria/Autriche

118 ORGANISATION: Österreichisches kommunalwissenschaftliches
     Dokumentationszentrum (KDZ)
     ADDRESS: A-1144 Wien, Linzerstrasse 452
     FIELDS COVERED: Public finances, economy, public utilities,
     communal matters, administration, regional studies, regional
     planning
     TYPE OF SERVICE: Written answers
     AVAILABILITY: General
     LANGUAGE(S): German
     CHARGES: None
     SIZE: Six staff

Belgium/Belgique

119 ORGANISATION: Centre belge d'Études et de Documentation des
     Eaux et de l'Air
     ADDRESS: Rue A. Stevart 2, 4000 Liège
     FIELDS COVERED: Chemistry of water, waste water, pollution of
     water and the atmosphere
     TYPE OF SERVICE: Information service (supply of photocopies,
     etc.); publications (periodical); study service
     AVAILABILITY: General
     LANGUAGE(S): Flemish and French (there are two centres, one
     for each)

120 ORGANISATION: Ministère des Travaux publics, Service de
     Documentation technique et des Études générales
     ADDRESS: Résidence Palace, rue de la Loi 155, 1040 Bruxelles
     FIELDS COVERED: Civil, public and administrative law; engineer-
     ing; architecture; urban planning

45

TYPE OF SERVICE: Library
AVAILABILITY: To personnel, and to members of the public for
   consultation
LANGUAGE(S): French, Flemish
SIZE, AND TYPE OF FILES: Card catalogues, periodicals. 16 staff
CURRENT SYSTEM: Manual

Canada

121 ORGANISATION: Intergovernmental Committee on Urban and
   Regional Research / Comité intergouvernemental de Recherches
   urbaines et régionales
   ADDRESS: 36 Wellesley Street West, Toronto, Ontario
   FIELDS COVERED: Urban and regional development, housing, local
   government, regional government, human resources, building
   research, transportation
   TYPE OF SERVICE: (1) clearing-house services; (2) technical
   information exchange services on housing and planning activities
   (weekly information summary cards sent out); (3) occasional
   reviews on specific housing and planning projects and programmes
   in Canada
   AVAILABILITY: Federal, provincial, territorial government services.
   Tendency towards more open access
   LANGUAGE(S): English, French
   CHARGES: None for all persons in government service
   CURRENT SYSTEM: Manual

122 ORGANISATION: Canadian Council on Urban and Regional
   Research
   ADDRESS: Suite 511, 151 Slater Street, Ottawa K1P 5H3
   TITLE OF SERVICE: *Urban and Regional References (URR)*
   FIELDS COVERED: Canadian urban affairs
   TYPE OF SERVICE: Bibliographical service; *URR* is a classified,
   indexed and annotated bibliography
   AVAILABILITY: General
   LANGUAGE(S): English, French
   CHARGES: Subscription
   SIZE, AND TYPE OF FILES: Magnetic tape of 10,000 items.
   Three staff
   CURRENT SYSTEM: Machine-based

46

Finland/Finlande

123 ORGANISATION: Tampere University of Technology, Library
   ADDRESS: Kirkkokatu 8, 33200 Tampere
   FIELDS COVERED: Town and country planning
   TYPE OF SERVICE: Inquiry service and maintenance of a central
      union catalogue of literature concerning town and country
      planning in Finnish research libraries. Bibliographies are published
      annually.
   AVAILABILITY: General
   LANGUAGE(S): Finnish
   CHARGES: None
   CURRENT SYSTEM: Manual

France

124 ORGANISATION: Centre d'Étude et de Recherche sur
      l'Administration économique et l'Aménagement du Territoire
   ADDRESS: Grenoble University, 38 St Martin
   TITLE OF SERVICE: Fichier de Documentation sur l'Aménagement
      du Territoire et de l'Action régionale
   FIELDS COVERED: Economics, geography, law, urbanism, sociology
      in relation to environmental planning
   TYPE OF SERVICE: Reference service
   AVAILABILITY: To researchers, administrators, Chambers of
      Commerce; available on subscription
   LANGUAGE(S): French
   CHARGES: Fr. 400 a year
   SIZE, AND TYPE OF FILES: 6,000 fiches a year
   CURRENT SYSTEM: Manual

125 ORGANISATION: Service technique central d'Amémagement
      urbain (STCAU)
   ADDRESS: 6 rue du Général Camou, Paris 7ᵉ
   TITLE OF SERVICE: Centre de Documentation sur l'Urbanisme
   FIELDS COVERED: Urbanism, particularly in relation to the
      social sciences
   TYPE OF SERVICE: Request services. *BULLDOC*: bulletin giving
      critical analyses on the level of knowledge rather than
      documentation. Interest profile service is envisaged

LANGUAGE(S): French
CHARGES: None at present
SIZE, AND TYPE OF FILES: 1,500 documents abstracted annually

Germany (Federal Republic)/République fédérale d'Allemagne

126 ORGANISATION: Institut für Raumordnung in der
Bundesforschungsanstalt für Landeskunde und Raumordnung
ADDRESS: Bonn/Bad Godesberg, Michaelshof
TITLE OF SERVICE: *Referateblatt zur Raumordnung*
FIELDS COVERED: Regional and country planning
TYPE OF SERVICE: Question answering
AVAILABILITY: General
LANGUAGE(S): German
CHARGES: None
CURRENT SYSTEM: Manual

International

127 ORGANISATION: Council of Europe
ADDRESS: Avenue de l'Europe, 67 Strasbourg, France
TITLE OF SERVICE: European Information Centre for Nature
Conservation
FIELDS COVERED: The natural environment in Europe, with
emphasis on improving it in view of its rapid deterioration
TYPE OF SERVICE: Clearing-house — shipments of environmental
documentation addressed to one contact per country in 30
countries. Documentation service. Publishes *Information Bulletin*
three times a year and *Newsletter* six times a year
AVAILABILITY: Directed both at particular persons and at the
wider public. General information service
LANGUAGE(S): English and French; summaries in German and
Italian in the *Information Bulletin; Newsletter* in these four
languages and in Turkish
CHARGES: None
SIZE, AND TYPE OF FILES: Documentation service — 500 books,
current periodicals 150 titles, 2,000 documents and pamphlets.
Clearing-house — approx. 1,000 documents circulated annually
CURRENT SYSTEM: Punched cards system with an alphabetical
index

128 ORGANISATION: International Federation for Housing and Planning/
Fédération internationale pour l'Habitation, l'Urbanisme et
l'Aménagement des Territoires/Internationaler Verband für
Wohnungswesen, Städtebau und Raumordnung
ADDRESS: Wassenaarseweg 43, 's Gravenhage, The Netherlands
TITLE OF SERVICE: Information services
FIELDS COVERED: Housing, planning, urban problems
TYPE OF SERVICE: Referral, bibliographical materials, accessions
lists
AVAILABILITY: Mainly to members
LANGUAGE(S): English, French, German
SIZE, AND TYPE OF FILES: Card indexes. Two staff
CURRENT SYSTEM: Manual

Italy/Italie

129 ORGANISATION: Centro di documentazione d'ingegneria civile e
planificazione territoriale
ADDRESS: Via de Togni 29, 20123 Milano
FIELDS COVERED: Civil engineering; architecture; national,
regional, urban planning; transport
TYPE OF SERVICE: (1) Three Roneo-typed periodical publications
— *Schede* (monthly), *Italian Planning Report* (bi-monthly in
English), *Documenti* (irregularly); (2) compilation and elaboration
of bibliographies; (3) research in Italian and foreign documents;
(4) technical translations; (5) photocopies
AVAILABILITY: General
LANGUAGE(S): Italian; English for the *Italian Planning Report*
CHARGES: Annual subscription Lire 20,000 (organisations, Lire
40,000). With the subscription one receives 12 numbers of *Schede*,
five numbers of *Documenti*, and can take advantage of the other
services offered by the Centre (prices vary according to the amount
of work involved)
SIZE, AND TYPE OF FILES: 50,000 abstracts (1970); 3,000
supplementary abstracts each year (of which 1,000 are published
in *Schede*)
CURRENT SYSTEM: Manual, own classification

130 ORGANISATION: Istituto di ricerca sulle acque del Consiglio
      Nazionale delle Ricerche
    ADDRESS: Via Reno 1, Roma
    FIELDS COVERED: Water pollution, desalination, hydrology,
      geo-hydrology
    TYPE OF SERVICE: Following up requests for information
    AVAILABILITY: On demand; also an SDI service operating in
      Italy
    LANGUAGE(S): Italian; summaries in English and Esperanto
    CHARGES: For monograph publications; otherwise none
    CURRENT SYSTEM: Peek-a-boo systems, UDC classification,
      thesaurus

Switzerland/Suisse

131 ORGANISATION: Institut für Orts-, Regional-und Landesplanung
      der Eidg. Technischen Hochschule
    ADDRESS: Weinbergstrasse 35, 8006 Zürich
    FIELDS COVERED: Environmental planning
    TYPE OF SERVICE: Oral and written information
    AVAILABILITY: To all subscribers
    LANGUAGE(S): German and French
    CHARGES: Information supplied free to institutions
    CURRENT SYSTEM: A computer-based system is planned

United Kingdom/Royaume-Uni

132 ORGANISATION: Centre for Environmental Studies
    ADDRESS: 5 Cambridge Terrace, Regent's Park, London NW1 4JL
    TITLE OF SERVICE: Library
    FIELDS COVERED: Planning, economics, quality of the environment
      transport, housing, poverty, commerce
    TYPE OF SERVICE: Reference service; loans
    AVAILABILITY: Open to public
    LANGUAGE(S): English
    SIZE, AND TYPE OF FILES: Card-index of books; index of
      periodicals. Two staff
    CURRENT SYSTEM: Manual

133 ORGANISATION: Council for the Protection of Rural England
ADDRESS: 4 Hobart Place, London SW1
FIELDS COVERED: Countryside, conservation
TYPE OF SERVICE: Acts as advisory and information centre
AVAILABILITY: General
LANGUAGE(S): English

134 ORGANISATION: National Housing and Town Planning Council Inc.
ADDRESS: 24 Devonshire Street, London W1
TITLE OF SERVICE: Publishes *Housing and Planning Yearbook*
FIELDS COVERED: Housing
TYPE OF SERVICE: Dissemination of information
LANGUAGE(S): English

Ergonomics/Ergonomie

United Kingdom/Royaume-Uni

135 ORGANISATION: Ergonomics Information Analysis Centre
ADDRESS: Department of Engineering Production, University of
Birmingham, Edgbaston, Birmingham 15
FIELDS COVERED: Ergonomics
TYPE OF SERVICE: Information and documentation services

Futurology/Futurologie

International

136 ORGANISATION: Association internationale FUTURIBLE
ADDRESS: 52 rue des Saints-Pères, 75 Paris 7e, France
TITLE OF SERVICE: Informations-Futurible
FIELDS COVERED: Futurology
TYPE OF SERVICE: Accumulation of information about documents
on futurology; establishment of indexes (dealing with articles,
courses, studies, etc.). Exchange of information: relevant
documents to interested persons; communication of references
AVAILABILITY: Specialised public (priority given to members
of the Association)
LANGUAGE(S): French (English being considered)
CHARGES: Subscription Fr. 165 a year
SIZE, AND TYPE OF FILES: 5,000–6,000 fiches
CURRENT SYSTEM: Traditional – author and subject indexes

Geography/Géographie

Canada

137 ORGANISATION: Arctic Institute of North America (AINA)
ADDRESS: 3458 Redpath Street, Montreal, PQ
TITLE OF SERVICE: Arctic Bibliography Project
FIELDS COVERED: Polar and subpolar regions and other areas with a cold climate; low-temperature science
TYPE OF SERVICE: Library collection in Montreal. Arctic Bibliography Project run from Washington DC. Abstracting and indexing of world literature on the polar and subpolar environments
AVAILABILITY: Library available generally
LANGUAGE(S): English
SIZE, AND TYPE OF FILES: At Montreal; 11,000 volumes; 20,000 pamphlets; manuscript field reports; maps; 800 current periodicals

France

138 ORGANISATION: Université de Bordeaux, Centre d'Études de Géographie tropicale
ADDRESS: Domaine universitaire, 33 Talence
FIELDS COVERED: Geography (physical, human, economic, with particular reference to the tropical humid zone)
TYPE OF SERVICE: Indexing and analysis; establishment of files for the service and of selective bibliographies; references furnished to researchers on demand. Various publications are envisaged
AVAILABILITY: Specialist public
LANGUAGE(S): French, English, Spanish, Portuguese, German, Italian, Dutch, Indonesian
CURRENT SYSTEM: Traditional

54

Germany (Federal Republic)/République fédérale d'Allemagne

139 ORGANISATION: Bundesforschungsanstalt für Landeskunde und
Raumordnung
ADDRESS: Bonn/Bad Godesberg, Michaelshof
TITLE OF SERVICE: *Documentatio Geographica*
FIELDS COVERED: Geography
TYPE OF SERVICE: Query answering
AVAILABILITY: General
LANGUAGE(S): German
CURRENT SYSTEM: Computerised

History/Histoire

140 ORGANISATION: University of Helsinki, Institute for Historical
    Research and Documentation
    ADDRESS: Meritullinkatu 14 A 4, 00170 Helsinki 17
    FIELDS COVERED: (1) History of Asia, Africa and Latin America
    (until now, mainly of Latin America); (2) history of Eastern
    Europe; (3) Scandinavian history; (4) history of Baltic lands
    TYPE OF SERVICE: Library co-ordination; research reviews
    (mimeo); documentation for studies on Eastern Europe, Latin
    America, Scandinavia and the Baltic area
    AVAILABILITY: General
    LANGUAGE(S): Finnish and Swedish
    CHARGES: None
    CURRENT SYSTEM: Manual

France

141 ORGANISATION: Centre de Recherches historiques
    ADDRESS: 54 boulevard Raspail, 75 Paris 6^e
    FIELDS COVERED: Economic and social history (France, Italy,
    Greece; 15th–20th centuries)
    TYPE OF SERVICE: Consultation of indexes; query answering
    service; lending
    AVAILABILITY: To specialists in particular
    LANGUAGE(S): French principally
    SIZE, AND TYPE OF FILES: For each project 3,000 to 100,000
    articles processed
    CURRENT SYSTEM: (1) Production of punched cards (FORCOD–
    FORTAB); (2) traditional system used for MS. index entries

142 ORGANISATION: Institut de Recherche et d'Histoire des
    Textes (IRHT)
    ADDRESS: 40 avenue d'Iéna, 75 Paris 16^e

FIELDS COVERED: Economic and social history of France in the
Middle Ages
TYPE OF SERVICE: Centre for exchanges and for references;
lending of microfilms
AVAILABILITY: Specialised public
LANGUAGE(S): French and Latin
CHARGES: Fr. 0·40 per loan of microfilm; Fr. 0·40 per enlargement
SIZE, AND TYPE OF FILES: Proper-name index — 350,000
references (35,000 a year). Subject index — 90,000 references
CURRENT SYSTEM: Indexes and descriptive notices of documents

International

143 ORGANISATION: International Institute of Social History/
Internationaal Instituut voor Sociale Geschiedenis/Institut
International d'Histoire sociale/Internationales Institut für
Sozialgeschichte
ADDRESS: Herengracht 262—266, Amsterdam-C, Netherlands
FIELDS COVERED: International social history
TYPE OF SERVICE: Query answering; preparation of
bibliographic materials for IISG publications only; consultation
of archival and reference material in reading room
AVAILABILITY: Restricted
LANGUAGE(S): English, French, German, Italian, Russian,
Serbo-Croat, Dutch, Spanish
CHARGES: Generally made only for photocopies and microcopies
SIZE, AND TYPE OF FILES: 400,000 books, approx. 1,600
current periodicals. Card indexes. About 16 staff
CURRENT SYSTEM: Manual

United Kingdom/Royaume-Uni

144 ORGANISATION: British Film Institute
ADDRESS: 81 Dean Street, London W1
TITLE OF SERVICE: Information Department
FIELDS COVERED: Film and television. Film archives
(National Film Archive)
LANGUAGE(S): English

Linguistics/Linguistique

United Kingdom/Royaume-Uni

145 ORGANISATION: The Institute of Linguists
ADDRESS: 91 Newington Causeway, London SE1
FIELDS COVERED: Information on linguists and linguistics
TYPE OF SERVICE: Information service to employers and public
AVAILABILITY: General
LANGUAGE(S): Various

Management

146 ORGANISATION: Österreichisches Produktivitätszentrum (ÖPZ)
ADDRESS: A-1014 Wien, Renngasse 5
TITLE OF SERVICE: ÖPZ – Anfragendienst
FIELDS COVERED: Economics, technology, political economy,
micro-economics, business administration
TYPE OF SERVICE: Query answering; expert opinions. Acts as a
referral centre
AVAILABILITY: General
LANGUAGE(S): German
CHARGES: Different, according to type of user
SIZE: Four staff; services of expert consultants available

147 ORGANISATION: Österreichisches Produktivitätszentrum (ÖPZ)
ADDRESS: A-1014 Wien, Renngasse 5
TITLE OF SERVICE: Technische Dokumentation
FIELDS COVERED: (1) Human engineering, human relations,
salary systems, industrial law; (2) management, organisation;
(3) accident prevention
TYPE OF SERVICE: Selective dissemination of information
AVAILABILITY: To all subscribers
LANGUAGE(S): German
CHARGES: AS 150 per subject per year
SIZE, AND TYPE OF FILES: 230 periodicals, 3,300 books,
100,000 documents

Germany (Federal Republic)/République fédérale d'Allemagne

148 ORGANISATION: Leitstelle Dokumentationsring
    Betriebswirtschaft
ADDRESS: Frankfurt, Gutleutstrasse 163–167, c/o RKW
TITLE OF SERVICE: Zeitschriften-Informationsdienst (ZID)
FIELDS COVERED: Management, economics
TYPE OF SERVICE: Query answering
AVAILABILITY: General
LANGUAGE(S): German
SIZE, AND TYPE OF FILES: 40,000 abstracts on cards DIN A6;
    30,000 titles on magnetic tape
CURRENT SYSTEM: Computerised

International

149 ORGANISATION: European Institute of Business Administration/
    Institut européen d'Administration des Affaires
ADDRESS: 77 boulevard de Constance, Fontainebleau, France
TITLE OF SERVICE: Library and documentation centre
FIELDS COVERED: Marketing management, financial management,
    statistics and operations research, personnel management,
    organisational behaviour, production management, general
    management, business policy, environmental management
TYPE OF SERVICE: Preparation of bibliographical materials;
    photocopying. Publishes *Management Documentation* (fortnightly
    bibliographical bulletin)
AVAILABILITY: *Management Documentation* by subscription
    (Fr. 270 a year)
LANGUAGE(S): French, English
CHARGES: See above
SIZE, AND TYPE OF FILES: Card indexes. Three professional staff

Ireland (Eire)/Irlande

150 ORGANISATION: Irish Management Institute
ADDRESS: 186 Orwell Road, Dublin 14
FIELDS COVERED: Management (also as applied to economics, psychology and education)
TYPE OF SERVICE: (1) Abstracting; (2) inquiry service; (3) selective dissemination of information; (4) provision of information in published form as a result of original research in management subjects
AVAILABILITY: Information service available to members as part of the services provided in return for membership fee
LANGUAGE(S): English
CHARGES: None to members
SIZE, AND TYPE OF FILES: Coverage of 250 journals; about 5,000 inquiries handled per year. SDI service given to about 40 executives. Three publications of original research, in survey form, are produced each year
CURRENT SYSTEM: (1) Manual—abstracts grouped by broad subject headings and by author; (2) Library service is provided for members of the Institute, and punched-card equipment is used to handle the integrated library and information system for information storage and retrieval purposes. Computer SDI for books is provided by way of MARC tapes held at Trinity College, Dublin

Italy/Italie

151 ORGANISATION: Centro di ricerche sull'impresa e lo sviluppo (CERIS)
ADDRESS: Via Ventimiglia 115, 10126 Torino
TITLE OF SERVICE: Programma SEDOC
FIELD COVERED: Management
TYPE OF SERVICE: Monthly abstracts; bibliographies; documentary research

152 ORGANISATION: Direzione del personale de La Rinascente-Upim
ADDRESS: Piazza Carlo Erba 6, 20100 Milano
TITLE OF SERVICE: Centro di documentazione e informazione
FIELDS COVERED: Management

TYPE OF SERVICE: Bibliographies, abstracts, photocopies.
Publishes a review containing a bibliographical index
AVAILABILITY: Particular and general
LANGUAGE(S): Italian
CHARGES: Not specified

153 ORGANISATION: IRI formazione e addestramento professionale
(IFAP)
ADDRESS: Piazza della Repubblica 59, 00185 Roma
TITLE OF SERVICE: Settore documentazione
FIELDS COVERED: Management; economic and social sciences
TYPE OF SERVICE: Bibliographies, abstracts, translations. Produces
Segnalazioni bibliografiche, a monthly in which abstracts and
descriptive fiches are published
AVAILABILITY: For specialists
LANGUAGE(S): Italian
CHARGES: On a fee-paying basis
SIZE, AND TYPE OF FILES: 5,500 books; 250 current subscript-
ions; 1,250 varied documents; seven business games
CURRENT SYSTEM: Manual; own classification

154 ORGANISATION: Istituto nazionale per l'incremento della
produttività (INIP)
ADDRESS: Piazza Independenza 11/B, 00185 Roma
FIELDS COVERED: Management
TYPE OF SERVICE: Bibliographies, consultation, photocopies
AVAILABILITY: General
LANGUAGE(S): Italian
CHARGES: On a fee-paying basis; sometimes free
SIZE, AND TYPE OF FILES: 2,500 books; 426 current subscriptions
CURRENT SYSTEM: Manual; own classification

155 ORGANISATION: Servizio documentazione CERIS (SEDOC),
Scuola di amministrazione industriale dell' Università di Torino
ADDRESS: Via Ventimiglia 115, 10126 Torino
TITLE OF SERVICE: Documentazione per le imprese
FIELDS COVERED: Management
TYPE OF SERVICE: 60—70 abstracts published each month
(*Panorama schede*, as supplement to the review *L'Impresa*);
1,700—2,000 descriptive fiches published eight times a year (as
supplement to the same review). Photocopies of the articles
described are available on demand

AVAILABILITY: General
LANGUAGE(S): Italian
CHARGES: Lire 100 per page photocopied
SIZE, AND TYPE OF FILES: 1,700–2,000 descriptive fiches every
two months
CURRENT SYSTEM: Double classification: (1) own classification
(keywords); (2) decimal classification, as used by the RKW of
Frankfurt

Netherlands/Pays-Bas

156 ORGANISATION: Nederlands Instituut voor Efficiency (NIVE)
ADDRESS: Parkstraat 18, 's Gravenhage
FIELDS COVERED: Management. Specialises in the possibilities
for the training of management personnel in the Netherlands and
in other countries (about 1,000 courses). Documentation on
other institutes in the field of management, Dutch and foreign
TYPE OF SERVICE: Information to individuals, in the form of
specially prepared bibliographies
AVAILABILITY: General
LANGUAGE(S): Dutch
CHARGES: None
SIZE: No information available
CURRENT SYSTEM: Classified by UDC; mechanisation considered

Sweden/Suède

157 ORGANISATION: Swedish Council for Personnel Administration
ADDRESS: Sturegatan 58, Box 5157, Stockholm
TITLE OF SERVICE: PADOC
FIELDS COVERED: Personnel administration; man at work; man
on the labour market. Emphasis is put on the behavioural science
aspect of these subjects, in particular on leadership, work adjust-
ment, training, organisational development, decision making,
vocational choice, counselling, adult education. The Council has
developed a data base and a system for information and
documentation covering subjects within its own field of activity.
The data base is connected to the library of the Council. For
some years, these activities have been at the development stage,

but the system is now in more permanent operation. Its aim is to provide all the necessary information for specialists, researchers and practitioners working within the field of personnel administration in its broadest sense

TYPE OF SERVICE:

(1)   Library service: lending, copies, circulation

(2)   Literature searches, query answering, preparation of bibliographical materials etc. are undertaken by documentalists

(3)   Selective dissemination of information according to profiles of interest

(4)   Print-out of literature searches

(5)   Consultation in documentation matters

(6)   Bibliographical journal with abstracts

AVAILABILITY: All services are available to the public

LANGUAGE(S): Scandinavian languages, English, German, French

CHARGES: Activities are subsidised by the Council, but additional charges are necessary

SIZE, AND TYPE OF FILES: The data base is stored on magnetic tape. The output consists of booklets of print-outs from the computer. Staff of six documentalists

CURRENT SYSTEM: Manual and computerised

Switzerland/Suisse

158   ORGANISATION: Bibliothek des betriebswissenschaftlichen Instituts der Eidg. Technischen Hochschule Zürich

ADDRESS: Zürichbergstrasse 18, 8028 Zürich

FIELDS COVERED: Industrial organisation

TYPE OF SERVICE: Produces bibliographical index cards — 40 per month

AVAILABILITY: To all subscribers

LANGUAGE(S): German

CHARGES: Switzerland — S Fr.55; abroad — S Fr.65

CURRENT SYSTEM: Manual; based on UDC

159   ORGANISATION: Centre d'Études industrielles (Centre for Education in International Management)

ADDRESS: 4 Chemin des Conches, 1211 Conches, Genève

TITLE OF SERVICE: Library

FIELDS COVERED: Business studies, management
TYPE OF SERVICE: Library and documentation service; information
to the institute and the local business community in Geneva

United Kingdom/Royaume-Uni

160 ORGANISATION: British Institute of Management
ADDRESS: Management House, Parker Street, London WC1
TITLE OF SERVICE: None
FIELDS COVERED: All aspects of management and management
training
TYPE OF SERVICE: Information service with reference and
lending library. Management Education Information Unit.
Publishes *Management Abstracts*
AVAILABILITY: Members only; certain publications generally
available
LANGUAGE(S): English

Political Science/
Sciences Politiques

161 ORGANISATION: Les Amitiés belgo-soviétiques (ABS)
ADDRESS: Rue du Méridien 21, 1030 Bruxelles
FIELDS COVERED: Relations between Belgium and the USSR
TYPE OF SERVICE: Information
AVAILABILITY: General
LANGUAGE(S): French, Flemish, Russian

162 ORGANISATION: Institut belge de Science politique/Belgisch
Instituut voor Wetenschap der Politiek (IBSP/BIWP)
ADDRESS: Rue des Champs Élysées 43, 1050 Bruxelles
FIELDS COVERED: Political science
TYPE OF SERVICE: Reference work, bibliographical research
AVAILABILITY: To personnel, and to members of the public with
authorisation
LANGUAGE(S): French, English
CHARGES: For photocopying; sometimes for other services
SIZE, AND TYPE OF FILES: Card catalogues (approx. 7,000 cards),
periodicals. Two staff
CURRENT SYSTEM: Manual

163 ORGANISATION: Union des Villes et Communes belges/Vereniging
van Belgische Steden en Gemeenten (UVCB/VBSG)
ADDRESS: Rue d'Arlon 53, 1040 Bruxelles
FIELDS COVERED: Administration and legal matters; public
administration
TYPE OF SERVICE: Query answering; inquiries; information
supplied to affiliated members; maintenance of
documentation files
AVAILABILITY: General
LANGUAGE(S): French, Flemish
CHARGES: For photocopying

SIZE, AND TYPE OF FILES: Card catalogues (approx. 67,500 items). Four staff
CURRENT SYSTEM: Manual

Canada

164 ORGANISATION: Canadian Institute of International Affairs
ADDRESS: Edgar Tarr House, 31 Wellesley St. East, Toronto M4Y 1G9, Ontario
FIELDS COVERED: Canadian external relations
TYPE OF SERVICE: Query answering; reference; preparation of bibliographies
AVAILABILITY: General
LANGUAGE(S): English
CHARGES: For borrowing (library membership costs $4·00 a year)
SIZE, AND TYPE OF FILES: Books, journals, newspaper-cuttings, UN documents (approx. 20,000 items). Two staff
CURRENT SYSTEM: Manual

Finland/Finlande

165 ORGANISATION: Finnish Institute of International Affairs
ADDRESS: Museokatu 18 A 9, 00100 Helsinki
FIELDS COVERED: Political science, social science
TYPE OF SERVICE: Inquiry service
AVAILABILITY: General
LANGUAGE(S): Finnish and Swedish
CHARGES: None
CURRENT SYSTEM: Traditional

France

166 ORGANISATION: The Atlantic Institute
ADDRESS: 120 rue de Longchamp, 75 Paris 16^e
TITLE OF SERVICE: Atlantic Institute Library
FIELDS COVERED: International affairs, military questions, economics, social affairs, politics
TYPE OF SERVICE: Being developed. Query answering and reference work; preparation of bibliographical materials
AVAILABILITY: General
LANGUAGE(S): English, French, German, Spanish
CHARGES: For photocopies and postal loans
SIZE, AND TYPE OF FILES: 4,500 books, 120 periodicals, 15,000 news-clippings (from 1969). 12 professional librarians
CURRENT SYSTEM: Manual

167 ORGANISATION: Université de Bordeaux, Institut d'Études politiques, Centre d'Étude et de Recherche sur la Vie locale
ADDRESS: Boîte postale 101, 33405 Talence
TITLE OF SERVICE: Library
FIELDS COVERED: Local political life, politics, and sociology
TYPE OF SERVICE: Reference facilities
AVAILABILITY: To students and researchers; to members of the public with authorisation
LANGUAGE(S): French, English
CHARGES: Carte de bibliothèque, Fr. 30
SIZE, AND TYPE OF FILES: Card indexes. 1,500 works, 200 periodicals. Two staff
CURRENT SYSTEM: Manual

Germany (Federal Republic)/République fédérale d'Allemagne

168 ORGANISATION: Leitstelle Politische Dokumentation
ADDRESS: 1 Berlin 45, Paulinenstrasse 22
TITLE OF SERVICE: (1) *Politische Dokumentation*; (2) *Politikwissenschaftliche Forschung*
FIELDS COVERED: Politics and political science
TYPE OF SERVICE: Query answering
AVAILABILITY: General
LANGUAGE(S): German
SIZE, AND TYPE OF FILES: 1,800 abstracts per year
CURRENT SYSTEM: Manual

169 ORGANISATION: Zentraldokumentation Parlamentsspiegel im
      Parlamentsarchiv des Landtags Nordrhein-Westfalen
   ADDRESS: Düsseldorf 1, Haus des Landtags
   TITLE OF SERVICE: Parlamentsspiegel—Kartei
   FIELDS COVERED: Law, policy
   TYPE OF SERVICE: Query answering
   AVAILABILITY: General
   LANGUAGE(S): German
   CHARGES: None
   SIZE, AND TYPE OF FILES: 37,000 cards (DIN A6) per year,
      with annual index
   CURRENT SYSTEM: Manual

International

170 ORGANISATION: Council of Europe
   ADDRESS: Avenue de l'Europe, 67 Strasbourg, France
   TITLE OF SERVICE: General Documentation Centre
   FIELDS COVERED: International relations (especially European
      aspects), public and international law, human rights, politics and
      government, economics
   TYPE OF SERVICE: Indexing of periodicals (card catalogue);
      compilation, on request, of bibliographies of articles from
      periodicals on given subjects
   AVAILABILITY: General
   LANGUAGE(S): Multilingual
   CHARGES: None
   SIZE, AND TYPE OF FILES: 500 periodicals indexed; approx.
      12,000 new entries added annually
   CURRENT SYSTEM: Own subject classification scheme

171 ORGANISATION: Council of Europe
   ADDRESS: Avenue de l'Europe, 67 Strasbourg, France
   TITLE OF SERVICE: Human Rights Library
   FIELDS COVERED: Human rights, public and international law,
      domestic legislation of member states of the European Convention
      on Human Rights
   TYPE OF SERVICE: Library service
   AVAILABILITY: To judges of the European Court of Human Rights,
      members of the Commission of Human Rights, members of the
      Secretariat, and persons doing research on human rights questions

LANGUAGE(S): Multilingual
CHARGES: None
SIZE, AND TYPE OF FILES: Approx. 3,000 volumes of books;
30 current periodical titles; approx. 15,000 UN documents and
printed publications concerning human rights
CURRENT SYSTEM: Classification by UDC

172 ORGANISATION: Council of Europe
ADDRESS: Avenue de l'Europe, 67 Strasbourg, France
TITLE OF SERVICE: Library
FIELDS COVERED: International relations (especially European
aspects), public and international law, politics and government,
economics, European history. Parliamentary documents of
member states; publications and documents of international
intergovernmental organisations
TYPE OF SERVICE: Library service; compilation, on request, of
bibliographies on specific subjects
AVAILABILITY: General
LANGUAGE(S): Multilingual
CHARGES: None
SIZE, AND TYPE OF FILES: Approx. 25,000 volumes; periodicals
(650 current titles); large collection of documents and printed
publications of international intergovernmental organisations
approx. 30,000 new entries each year
CURRENT SYSTEM: Modified UDC

173 ORGANISATION: European Consortium for Political Research
ADDRESS: Gamle Kalvedalsvei 12, 5,000 Bergen, Norway
TITLE OF SERVICE: Data information service
FIELDS COVERED: Political science, political sociology
TYPE OF SERVICE: Newsletters, guides to data-generation efforts
in Europe and to data sets on European politics
AVAILABILITY: To members of ECPR ($1,000 a year for a large
package of services). Central headquarters located at University
of Essex, Colchester, England
LANGUAGE(S): English
CHARGES: None to members
SIZE, AND TYPE OF FILES: Approx. 4,000—5,000 data
documents (codebooks, etc.)
CURRENT SYSTEM: Not yet computerised

174 ORGANISATION: Institut International d'Administration publique
ADDRESS: 2 avenue de l'Observatoire, Paris, France
TITLE OF SERVICE: Centre de Recherche et de Documentation sur la Fonction publique
FIELDS COVERED: Public administration in France and elsewhere; comparative studies in public administration
TYPE OF SERVICE: Abstracting the literature; bibliographical research; publication of *Annuaire International de la Fonction Publique*
AVAILABILITY: To members of the public with authorisation
LANGUAGE(S): French
CHARGES: For reprographic work
SIZE, AND TYPE OF FILES: Card catalogues of abstracts, etc. Two staff
CURRENT SYSTEM: Manual

175 ORGANISATION: International Institute of Administrative Sciences
ADDRESS: Rue de la Charité 25, 1040 Bruxelles, Belgium
TITLE OF SERVICE: Information and research service
FIELDS COVERED: Public administration
TYPE OF SERVICE: Query answering and reference work; preparation of bibliographical materials
AVAILABILITY: Restricted to students and research workers
LANGUAGE(S): French and English
CHARGES: For photocopies; charge also possible if extensive work involved
SIZE, AND TYPE OF FILES: Books and journals, mimeographed documents, card indexes (approx. 300,000 cards). Five staff
CURRENT SYSTEM: Manual

176 ORGANISATION: International Political Science Association
ADDRESS: Rue des Champs Élysées 43, 1050 Bruxelles, Belgium
TITLE OF SERVICE: *International Political Science Abstracts*
FIELDS COVERED: Political science, international relations
TYPE OF SERVICE: Abstracting service
AVAILABILITY: To subscribers
LANGUAGE(S): French and English
CHARGES: Subscription

Ireland (Eire)/Irlande

177 ORGANISATION: Institute of Public Administration (An Foras Riarchain)
ADDRESS: 59 Lansdowne Road, Dublin 4
FIELDS COVERED: Public administration; social administration and related subjects, including political science
TYPE OF SERVICE: Library, query answering, reference work, preparation of bibliographies, literature searches. Referral service to staff members
AVAILABILITY: To members of the Institute, individual and corporate. General public may use reading room for reference
LANGUAGE(S): English, French (spoken by some staff)
CHARGES: Corporate membership fee by arrangement; individual membership fee £8·00 a year (£6·00 to public service employees)
SIZE, AND TYPE OF FILES: 10,000 books, 170 periodicals, annual reports, abstracts. Staff comprises two qualified librarians and one information officer
CURRENT SYSTEM: Manual

Italy/Italie

178 ORGANISATION: Istituto affari internazionali (IAI), Library
ADDRESS: Viale Mazzini 88, 00195 Roma
TITLE OF SERVICE: None
FIELDS COVERED: International relations; politics outside Italy
TYPE OF SERVICE: Bibliographical service; preparation of bibliographies; photocopies; translation. *L'Italia nella politica internazionale* is published quarterly and distributed to subscribers only
LANGUAGE(S): Italian and English
CHARGES: For the publication Lire 9,500; for other services appropriate fees charged
SIZE, AND TYPE OF FILES: 20,000 volumes and documents, 300 periodicals
CURRENT SYSTEM: Manual; own classification

179 ORGANISATION: Istituto per la documentazione giuridica del Consiglio Nazionale delle Ricerche
ADDRESS: Via Panciatichi 56/16, 50127 Firenze

FIELDS COVERED: Law
TYPE OF SERVICE: Bibliographical publications on demand
AVAILABILITY: General
LANGUAGE(S): Italian
CURRENT SYSTEM: Manual and machine-based

180 ORGANISATION: Istituto per le scienze della amministrazione
    pubblica (ISAP), Library
    ADDRESS: Via Marozzo della Rocca 9, 20123 Milano
    FIELDS COVERED: Public law
    TYPE OF SERVICE: Consultation of documents; exchange of
    publications and information
    AVAILABILITY: General
    LANGUAGE(S): Italian
    CHARGES: On a fee-paying basis
    CURRENT SYSTEM: Manual; own classification

181 ORGANISATION: Laboratorio di studi sulla ricerca e sulla
    documentazione del Consiglio Nazionale delle Ricerche
    ADDRESS: Via Cesare de Lollis 12, Roma
    FIELDS COVERED: Political science
    TYPE OF SERVICE: Information service
    AVAILABILITY: General
    LANGUAGE(S): Italian, French and English
    CURRENT SYSTEM: Manual

Netherlands/Pays-Bas

182 ORGANISATION: Instituut voor Bestuurswetenschappen
    ADDRESS: Sir Winston Churchill Laan 275, Rijswijk (Z-H)
    FIELDS COVERED: Public administration — administrative
    organisation, local government law, government grants and
    subsidies, administrative aspects of environment protection,
    personnel administration, education instruction, and administrative
    officers, public finance, planning and management, budgeting
    systems (PPBS) at local government level
    TYPE OF SERVICE: Limited — preparation of bibliographical
    material, literature searches
    AVAILABILITY: Restricted to government institutions, universities,
    professional organisations, etc. Service to private persons only in
    exceptional cases

LANGUAGE(S): Dutch. Short communications in English, French and German

CHARGES: According to time required to complete investigation

SIZE, AND TYPE OF FILES: Books and journals; card index on problems covering regional government. 1,000 books, 100 journals. No special information staff; about 14 staff engaged in research organisation and education

CURRENT SYSTEM: Manual

183 ORGANISATION: Ministerie van Buitenlandse Zaken, Afdeling Documentatie

ADDRESS: Muzenstraat 30, 's Gravenhage

FIELDS COVERED: Political science. Service activities are concentrated in the field of development problems

TYPE OF SERVICE: Mostly the user is supplied with the literature that answers his questions. Sometimes bibliographies are specially prepared

AVAILABILITY: General (clients are often students)

LANGUAGE(S): Dutch, English, French, German

SIZE: Growing

CURRENT SYSTEM: Manual; classification by UDC

Sweden/Suède

184 ORGANISATION: Swedish Institute of International Affairs (Archives Section)

ADDRESS: Wennergren Center, Sveavägen 166, S113 46 Stockholm

TITLE OF SERVICE: *Archives*

FIELDS COVERED: Foreign policy

TYPE OF SERVICE: Press-cutting service, etc.

AVAILABILITY: To subscribers

185 ORGANISATION: The Africa Bureau
ADDRESS: 2 Arundel Street, London WC2
FIELDS COVERED: African affairs; British public opinion on Africa
TYPE OF SERVICE: Information and referral

186 ORGANISATION: European Communities Press and Information Office
ADDRESS: 23 Chesham Street, London SW1
FIELDS COVERED: European communities, European integration
TYPE OF SERVICE: Information service; contacts with media
LANGUAGE(S): Various

187 ORGANISATION: Institute of Local Government Studies (INLOGOV), University of Birmingham
ADDRESS: PO Box 363, Birmingham B15 2TT
TITLE OF SERVICE: Corporate Planning Information Service
FIELDS COVERED: Local and central government (UK) activity in the field of planning, programming, budgeting systems (PPBS), corporate planning, corporate management
TYPE OF SERVICE: Preparation of biennial bibliographies; studies of individual local authorities; abstracts (1970–72 only); query answering
AVAILABILITY: General
LANGUAGE(S): English
CHARGES: Annual subscription £5·00
SIZE, AND TYPE OF FILES: Books, reports, articles, etc., held in the Institute. One part-time member of staff
CURRENT SYSTEM: Manual

188 ORGANISATION: Government of Northern Ireland
ADDRESS: Stormont Castle, Belfast BT4 3ST
TITLE OF SERVICE: Government Information Service
FIELDS COVERED: Government and activities in Northern Ireland
TYPE OF SERVICE: Information, publicity
AVAILABILITY: Publications and releases to the media
LANGUAGE(S): English

189 ORGANISATION: Royal Institute of International Affairs
ADDRESS: Chatham House, St. James's Square, London SW1
FIELDS COVERED: Politics and international affairs
TYPE OF SERVICE: Library

190 ORGANISATION: University of Edinburgh, Centre for European
Governmental Studies
ADDRESS: Old College, South Bridge, Edinburgh
FIELDS COVERED: Europe and European communities
TYPE OF SERVICE: Limited information service
LANGUAGE(S): Various

Psychology/Psychologie

Belgium/Belgique

191 ORGANISATION: Centre médico-psycho-pédagogique
   ADDRESS: Rue Pierre Decoster 115, 1190 Bruxelles
   FIELDS COVERED: Child psychology, educational psychology,
      guidance, educational and vocational training
   TYPE OF SERVICE: Documentation service
   AVAILABILITY: To personnel, and to members of the public with
      authorisation
   LANGUAGE(S): French, Flemish
   CHARGES: None
   SIZE, AND TYPE OF FILES: Card catalogues. Six staff
   CURRENT SYSTEM: Manual

192 ORGANISATION: Séminaire d'Orientation scolaire et
      professionnelle de l'Université de Liège
   ADDRESS: Boulevard Pierrecot 36, 4000 Liège
   FIELDS COVERED: Applied psychology
   TYPE OF SERVICE: Bibliographical research
   AVAILABILITY: To personnel, and to members of the public with
      authorisation
   LANGUAGE(S): French
   CHARGES: None
   SIZE, AND TYPE OF FILES: Card catalogues (books, journals,
      memoirs, theses). Three staff
   CURRENT SYSTEM: Manual

193 ORGANISATION: Central Medical Library of Finland
ADDRESS: Haartmaninkatu 4, 00290 Helsinki
FIELDS COVERED: Psychology in connection with medicine
TYPE OF SERVICE: Selective dissemination of information, and
retrospective searches
AVAILABILITY: General
LANGUAGE(S): Finnish and Swedish, and English when based on
MEDLARS
CHARGES: For SDI service 300 Finnish marks (MEDLARS
retrospective search per year) or 5 Finnish marks (manual search
per year)
CURRENT SYSTEM: Both manual and computerised

France

194 ORGANISATION: Centre international de l'Enfance (CIE)
ADDRESS: Chateau de Longchamp, 75 Paris 16^e
FIELDS COVERED: Psychology (since 1950); medico-social view of
childhood
TYPE OF SERVICE: List of acquisitions, bibliographies on special
subjects, and photocopies of articles supplied on demand;
publishes bibliographies, guides, indexes, etc.
AVAILABILITY: General
LANGUAGE(S): Various
CHARGES: Complete subscription for all references — Fr. 800;
partial subscription — entry fee of Fr. 20, plus expenses
SIZE, AND TYPE OF FILES: 880 periodicals, 12,500 works (700
titles added each year)
CURRENT SYSTEM: Traditional; classification (modified for the
needs of the Centre) by Eileen Cunningham

Italy/Italie

195 ORGANISATION: Istituto della Psicologia del Consiglio Nazionale delle Ricerche
ADDRESS: Via dei Monti Tiburtini 509, 00157 Roma
FIELDS COVERED: Psycho-physiology; comparative psychology, cognitive processes, social interaction processes; psycho-pedagogy
TYPE OF SERVICE: Information service
AVAILABILITY: General
LANGUAGE(S): Italian
SIZE: National importance; has relations with international organisations
CURRENT SYSTEM: Manual

United Kingdom/Royaume-Uni

196 ORGANISATION: National Institute of Industrial Psychology
ADDRESS: 14 Welbeck Street, London W1M 8DR
FIELDS COVERED: Occupational psychology
TYPE OF SERVICE: Inquiry service. Loans through British Library (Lending Division), Bulletins, annual reports, and research reports
AVAILABILITY: General
LANGUAGE(S): English
SIZE, AND TYPE OF FILES: 6,000 books, 10,000 pamphlets, 130 current periodicals
CURRENT SYSTEM: Traditional

Social and Behavioural Sciences/ Sciences Sociales et Sciences du Comportement

Austria/Autriche

197 ORGANISATION: Guardaval Vereinigung zur Herausgabe von
Zeitungen und Zeitschriften, GmbH
ADDRESS: A-1010 Wien, Rosendorferstrasse
TITLE OF SERVICE: *Guarda-Österreichs-Dokumentation*
FIELDS COVERED: Administration, politics, economics, culture,
social affairs, integration, education
TYPE OF SERVICE: Information service
AVAILABILITY: For subscribers to the journal *Guarda-Österreichs-Dokumentation*
LANGUAGE(S): German
CHARGES: None to subscribers

Belgium/Belgique

198 ORGANISATION: Bibliothèque Lionel Bertelson, ASBL
ADDRESS: Maison de la Presse, Petite rue au Beurre 4, 1000
Bruxelles
FIELDS COVERED: The press; history of journalism, work of
journalists in Belgium
TYPE OF SERVICE: Bibliographical research
AVAILABILITY: General
LANGUAGE(S): French
CHARGES: None
SIZE, AND TYPE OF FILES: Catalogues. One member of staff

199 ORGANISATION: Centre de Documentation et de Recherches
sociales (CEDORES)
ADDRESS: Avenue Meurée 39, 6001 Marcinelle

FIELDS COVERED: Social sciences
TYPE OF SERVICE: Query answering, inquiries, reference work,
bibliographical research
AVAILABILITY: General
LANGUAGE(S): French, English, German
CHARGES: None
SIZE, AND TYPE OF FILES: Card catalogues, periodicals.
Machine-readable data to be introduced. Seven staff
CURRENT SYSTEM: Manual and automatic

200 ORGANISATION: Centre d'Étude des Problèmes des Pays en
Développement de l'Université de Liège (CEDEV)
ADDRESS: Place du 20 Août 13–15, 4000 Liège
FIELDS COVERED: Development
TYPE OF SERVICE: Inquiries, documentation, information
AVAILABILITY: To personnel, and to members of the public with
authorisation
SIZE, AND TYPE OF FILES: Card catalogues (approx. 100,000
entries), periodicals. One member of staff
CURRENT SYSTEM: Manual

201 ORGANISATION: Centre d'Études américaines / Center for
American Studies (CEA/CAS)
ADDRESS: Boulevard de l'Empereur 4, 1000 Bruxelles
FIELDS COVERED: American studies
TYPE OF SERVICE: Wide range of bibliographical assistance
AVAILABILITY: General
LANGUAGE(S): English, French, Flemish
CHARGES: For reproduction; otherwise none
SIZE, AND TYPE OF FILES: Card catalogues. Five to six staff
CURRENT SYSTEM: Manual

202 ORGANISATION: Centre national pour l'Étude des États de l'Est
ADDRESS: Avenue Jeanne 44, 1050 Bruxelles
FIELDS COVERED: Specialised documentation on political, social,
economic and legal matters relating to the socialist countries of
Europe and Asia
TYPE OF SERVICE: Library. Analysis of articles in periodicals;
preparation of summaries
AVAILABILITY: General
LANGUAGE(S): French, English, German, Flemish, Russian, etc.

CHARGES: For photocopying
SIZE, AND TYPE OF FILES: Card catalogues (approx. 400,000
    entries). 10 staff
CURRENT SYSTEM: Manual

203 ORGANISATION: Centre pour l'Étude des Problèmes du Monde
    musulman contemporain
    ADDRESS: Avenue Jeanne 44, 1050 Bruxelles
    FIELDS COVERED: Current affairs, culture, religion, economics,
        politics, geography, history, sociology, fine arts
    TYPE OF SERVICE: Library and information
    AVAILABILITY: General
    LANGUAGE(S): French
    SIZE, AND TYPE OF FILES: 40,000 card entries. Seven staff
    CURRENT SYSTEM: Manual

204 ORGANISATION: Institut belge d'Information et de Documentation
    (INBEL)
    ADDRESS: Rue Montoyer 3, 1040 Bruxelles
    FIELDS COVERED: Information and documentation on Belgium
        and the techniques of mass communication
    TYPE OF SERVICE: Abstracting; acquisition of basic materials
    AVAILABILITY: Restricted; to the public only if authorised
    LANGUAGE(S): French, Flemish
    SIZE, AND TYPE OF FILES: Card catalogues; approx. 2,000
        books; periodicals. Three staff
    CURRENT SYSTEM: Manual

205 ORGANISATION: Institut de Sociologie, Library
    ADDRESS: Avenue Jeanne 44, 1050 Bruxelles
    FIELDS COVERED: Social sciences, politics, economics
    TYPE OF SERVICE: Bibliographical research
    AVAILABILITY: Students and researchers
    LANGUAGE(S): French
    CHARGES: For photocopying
    SIZE, AND TYPE OF FILES: Card catalogues (440 drawers),
        periodicals, bibliographies. Eight staff
    CURRENT SYSTEM: Manual

206 ORGANISATION: Ministère de la Défense nationale, Centre de
    Documentation et Bibliothèque centrale (ACDB)
    ADDRESS: Rue des Petits Carmes 22, 1000 Bruxelles

FIELDS COVERED: Science and technology, social sciences
TYPE OF SERVICE: Bibliographical research
AVAILABILITY: To ministry staff
LANGUAGE(S): French, Flemish
CHARGES: For photocopying
SIZE, AND TYPE OF FILES: Card catalogues, periodicals.
  Nine staff
CURRENT SYSTEM: Manual

207 ORGANISATION: Sénat – Services d'Étude et de Documentation
ADDRESS: Place de la Nation, 1000 Bruxelles
FIELDS COVERED: In particular public law, but also all areas of
  work dealt with by the Senate
TYPE OF SERVICE: Query answering, reference work, bibliograph-
  ical research
AVAILABILITY: To personnel, and to members of the public with
  authorisation
LANGUAGE(S): French, Flemish, English
SIZE, AND TYPE OF FILES: Card catalogue (approx. 160,000
  items), periodicals. 14 staff
CURRENT SYSTEM: Manual

208 ORGANISATION: USIS (United States Information Service),
  American Library
ADDRESS: Square du Bastion 1c, 1050 Bruxelles
TITLE OF SERVICE: USIS
FIELDS COVERED: American studies
TYPE OF SERVICE: Reference services
AVAILABILITY: General
LANGUAGE(S): English, French, Flemish
CHARGES: For photocopying

209 ORGANISATION: Carleton University
ADDRESS: Department of Sociology and Anthropology,
Ottawa K1S 5B6, Ontario
TITLE OF SERVICE: Social Science Data Library (Archive) (SSDA)
FIELDS COVERED: Social sciences, particularly sociology, political
science, anthropology, demography
TYPE OF SERVICE: (1) Data depository for Carleton University
social science departments; (2) documentation and dissemination
centre; (3) liaison between data banks
AVAILABILITY: Requests considered on an individual basis
LANGUAGE(S): English
SIZE, AND TYPE OF FILES: Survey archives; textual materials;
access to materials held by Inter-University Consortium for
Political Research
CURRENT SYSTEM: Computer-based

210 ORGANISATION: Institute for Behavioural Research Data Bank
ADDRESS: IBR, York University, 4700 Keele Street, Downsview,
Ontario
FIELDS COVERED: Social psychology, political science, sociology,
urban studies, social science
TYPES OF SERVICE: (1) Data clearing-house, (2) information
retrieval, (3) data dissemination, from (a) Canadian Attitude and
Behaviour Archive, (b) Cross-Cultural/Cross-National Archive,
(c) Canadian Census Data Base
AVAILABILITY: Mainly to researchers (except to those working
for secret purposes, or for financial or political gain). Fifteen per
cent of holdings restricted to University members
LANGUAGE(S): English
CHARGES: Information and data searches $10; individual data
sets and codebooks on tape $50–100; standard census summary
tape $50; custom summary census data – cost on request
CURRENT SYSTEM: Computerised

211 ORGANISATION: National Library of Canada
ADDRESS: Reference Branch (CAN/SDI), National Library, 395
Wellington Street, Ottawa K1A 0N4, Ontario
TITLE OF SERVICE: CAN/SDI (Humanities and Social Sciences)
FIELDS COVERED: Social sciences

TYPE OF SERVICE: Information retrieval system based on
available machine readable bibliographical data, e.g. ASCA V,
MARC II, ERIC
AVAILABILITY: To subscribers
LANGUAGE(S): Various
CHARGES: Base fee $40
TYPE OF FILES: Based on commercially available machine readable
data files
CURRENT SYSTEM: Computer-based

212 ORGANISATION: Parliament of Canada
ADDRESS: Parliament Buildings, Ottawa 4, Ontario
TITLE OF SERVICE: Library of Parliament
FIELDS COVERED: Subjects of interest to the Canadian
Parliament, especially economics, finance, law, politics, social
welfare and Canadiana
TYPE OF SERVICE: Information services and bibliographical
research facilities
AVAILABILITY: Primarily intended for members of the Canadian
Parliament
LANGUAGE(S): English, French
SIZE, AND TYPE OF FILES: 350,000 books, 1,720 periodicals,
700 newspapers, 1,500 reels microfilm
CURRENT SYSTEM: Manual

213 ORGANISATION: Université de Montreal, Centre de Sondage
(Survey Research Centre)
ADDRESS: Case Postale 6128, Montreal 101
FIELDS COVERED: Social sciences (sociology, political science,
demography, communology) and other fields in which social-
survey methods are applicable (geography, education, law, etc.).
Most material relates to the Province of Quebec, with some cross-
Canada surveys in collaboration with the Survey Research Centre,
York University
TYPE OF SERVICE: (1) Data bank providing access to local and
other Canadian centres data; (2) Consultation on research design
and methodology; (3) sampling, questionnaire design and
translation, field work, coding, data analysis; (4) guide to holdings
produced
AVAILABILITY: Generally unrestricted for academic use, subject
to confidentiality controls

LANGUAGE(S): French and English, but primarily French
CHARGES: Cost, plus 30 per cent for overheads (subject to revision)
SIZE, AND TYPE OF FILES: Data bank, 12—15 data sets (by mid-1974); technical documentation. Two data-bank staff
CURRENT SYSTEM: Manual and machine-based

Finland/Finlande

214 ORGANISATION: Library of Parliament
ADDRESS: Eduskuntatalo, 00102 Helsinki
FIELDS COVERED: Social sciences, political science, environmental planning
TYPE OF SERVICE: Inquiry service and searches on demand; publishes *Valtion Virallisjulkaisut*, an annual bibliography of Finnish government publications
AVAILABILITY: General
LANGUAGE(S): Finnish and Swedish
CHARGES: Usually none
CURRENT SYSTEM: Manual; computerisation planned

France

215 ORGANISATION: Centre de Documentation Israël et Moyen-Orient
ADDRESS: 19 boulevard Poissonnière, 75 Paris 9ᵉ
FIELDS COVERED: Social sciences
TYPE OF SERVICE: Acquisition, conservation and communication of documents (on loan); indexing and analysis, and establishment of catalogues. Dissemination of information: query answering (most questions come from abroad, principally from Israel). Reproduction service
AVAILABILITY: General
LANGUAGE(S): English, French, German, Hebrew
CHARGES: For photocopies (Fr. 0·75) and loans (Fr. 10 deposit)
SIZE, AND TYPE OF FILES: 700 works, 80 periodicals
CURRENT SYSTEM: Traditional

216 ORGANISATION: Centre d'Études indiennes de Sciences sociales, Laboratoire du CNRS
ADDRESS: 54 boulevard Raspail, 75 Paris 6ᵉ

FIELDS COVERED: Social sciences
TYPE OF SERVICE: Acquisition, conservation and communication of documents; analysis and indexing of documents and establishment of catalogues; dissemination of information – furnishing of references on request; dissemination of acquisition list
AVAILABILITY: Specialist public
LANGUAGE(S): English principally; also Sanskrit and modern Indian languages
SIZE, AND TYPE OF FILES: Author index, 15,000 references; subject index, over 15,000 references. About 6,000 works (1,000–1,200 a year); 74 periodicals (India, Pakistan, England, USA, France); 30 rolls of microfilm; 40 maps
CURRENT SYSTEM: Traditional

217 ORGANISATION: Fondation nationale des Sciences politiques
ADDRESS: 27 rue Saint-Guillaume, 75 Paris 7^e
TITLE OF SERVICE: Centre de Documentation contemporaine
FIELDS COVERED: The social sciences applied to political, economic and social problems of the world today
TYPE OF SERVICE: Supply of bibliographical references by subject, and, on demand, copies of documents
AVAILABILITY: To students and researchers
LANGUAGE(S): French
CHARGES: None for bibliographical references; cost price for reproductions
SIZE, AND TYPE OF FILES: 350,000 references (1970); 2,000 supplementary references every month
CURRENT SYSTEM: Manual

218 ORGANISATION: Institut d'Études slaves
ADDRESS: 9 rue Michelet, 75 Paris 6^e
FIELDS COVERED: Social sciences (Slav countries, Central Europe and the Balkans)
TYPE OF SERVICE: Acquisition, conservation and communication of documents; query answering by telephone (occasionally). Publications: one current bibliographical review of works (from all over the world) relating to Slavistics; specialist bibliographies
AVAILABILITY: Specialist public
LANGUAGE(S): Various
SIZE, AND TYPE OF FILES: 50,850 works, 300 periodicals
CURRENT SYSTEM: Traditional

219 ORGANISATION: Maison des Sciences de l'Homme (MSH)
ADDRESS: 54 boulevard Raspail, 75 Paris 6^e
TITLE OF SERVICE: Service d'Échange d'Informations scientifiques
FIELDS COVERED: Social and behavioural sciences (exchange of information relating to the science of man, particularly as regards the trends of research — language and methods, documentary tools, institutions and researchers, scientific policy)
TYPE OF SERVICE: Information exchange service; building up of collections. Publications are based on the five series A — Bibliographies; B — Guides et répertoires; C — Catalogues et inventaires; D — Méthodes et techniques; E — Terminologie
AVAILABILITY: General
LANGUAGE(S): French
CHARGES: Varies with each volume
CURRENT SYSTEM: Processing by computer is planned

220 ORGANISATION: METRA Internationale, Societé d'Études et de Mathématiques appliquées (SEMA)
ADDRESS: 9 rue Georges Picard, 75 Paris 15^e
FIELDS COVERED: Social sciences; psycho-sociology
TYPE OF SERVICE: Documents collection, relating to investigations by the SOFRES (Société Française d'Enquêtes par Sondage); inquiry service in connection with completed studies; publication of annual indexes, listing studies completed during the year
AVAILABILITY: General
LANGUAGE(S): Various
CHARGES: Vary according to subscription
CURRENT SYSTEM: Traditional

221 ORGANISATION: Office de la Recherche scientifique et technique outre-mer (ORSTOM)
ADDRESS: 70—74 route d'Aubray, 93140 Bondy (Service central de Documentation); 24 rue Bayard, 75008 Paris (Direction générale)
TITLE OF SERVICE: Service central de Documentation
FIELDS COVERED: Sociology, social psychology, economics, demography, geography, ethnology, linguistics, archaeology, history
TYPE OF SERVICE: Management, production and dissemination of documentation. Preparation of two-yearly bibliography, and of specialised bibliographies. Loan of library materials
AVAILABILITY: Primarily to personnel, but also to the public

LANGUAGE(S): French, English
CHARGES: Some; catalogue of publications is available free
SIZE, AND TYPE OF FILES: Card indexes of books and periodicals.
  Total of six library staff
CURRENT SYSTEM: Manual

Germany (Federal Republic)/République fédérale d'Allemagne

222 ORGANISATION: Deutsches Institut für Afrika-Forschung e.V.
  ADDRESS: 2 Hamburg 36, Neuer Jungfernstieg 21
  TITLE OF SERVICE: Dokumentations—Leitstelle Afrika
  FIELDS COVERED: Social sciences related to social and economic
    development of Africa
  TYPE OF SERVICE: Query answering and reference work,
    reference service, literature searches, preparation of bibliographical
    materials
  AVAILABILITY: Generally unrestricted
  LANGUAGE(S): German
  CHARGES: Restitution of material cost. Subscription to
    Dokumentationsdienst Afrika, DM 10 per copy
  SIZE, AND TYPE OF FILES: Card indexes. Six full-time staff
  CURRENT SYSTEM: Manual; uses *Thesaurus für wirtschaftliche und
    soziale Entwicklung* ('Thesaurus for economic and social
    development')

223 ORGANISATION: Informationszentrum für sozialwissenschaftliche
    Forschung bei der Arbeitsgemeinschaft Sozialwissenschaftsinstitute
    e.V. (Information Centre for Research in the Social Sciences of
    the Association of Social Science Institutes)
  ADDRESS: 53 Bonn/Bad Godesberg, Plittersdorfer Strasse 21
    (telephone: 0221/362 600)
  FIELDS COVERED: Social sciences; in particular sociology, political
    sciences, economics, psychology, social psychology, ethnology,
    anthropology, education
  TYPE OF SERVICE: (1) publication of annual surveys of
    completed, current and planned research and development
    projects; (2) query answering (computer-based from 1974)
  AVAILABILITY: Unrestricted
  LANGUAGE(S): German

CHARGES: For publications (including *Forschungsarbeiten in den Sozialwissenschaften* – DM30)
SIZE, AND TYPE OF FILES: (1) Card index of social research establishments in German-speaking countries (2,000 entries); (2) files of questionnaires (approx. 3,000 handled each year). 10–15 staff (four engaged in information activities)
CURRENT SYSTEM: Computer-based from mid-1973 onwards

224 ORGANISATION: Institut für Ibero-Amerika Kunde
ADDRESS: 2 Hamburg 36, Alsterglacis 8
TITLE OF SERVICE: Dokumentations-Leitstelle Lateinamerika
FIELDS COVERED: Social sciences related to social and economic development of Latin America
TYPE OF SERVICE: Query answering and reference work, referral searches, literature searches, preparation of bibliographical materials. Publications include *Dokumentationsdienst Latein-amerika* and *Informationsdienst der ADLAF*
AVAILABILITY: Unrestricted
LANGUAGE(S): German
CHARGES: Restitution of material costs. Annual subscription to *Dokumentationsdienst Lateinamerika*, $10
SIZE, AND TYPE OF FILES: Card indexes (DIN A6 – 14·8 x 10·4 cm). Eight full-time staff
CURRENT SYSTEM: Uses a thesaurus prepared by the West German documentation centre for developing countries (Stiftung Deutsches Übersee-Institut)

225 ORGANISATION: Stiftung Deutsches Übersee-Institut
ADDRESS: 2 Hamburg 36, Neuer Jungfernstieg 21
TITLE OF SERVICE: Dokumentation
FIELDS COVERED: Economics, educational and sociological aspects of developing and overseas countries (through the documentation departments of the Institut für Asienkunde; Institut für Ibero-Amerika Kunde; Deutsches Orient-Institut; Deutsches Institut für Afrika-Forschung)
TYPE OF SERVICE: Query answering
AVAILABILITY: General
LANGUAGE(S): German
CHARGES: None
SIZE: Approx. 100,000 titles
CURRENT SYSTEM: Manual

226 ORGANISATION: International Labour Office (ILO)
ADDRESS: 1211 Genève 22, Switzerland
TITLE OF SERVICE: Integrated Scientific Information
Service (ISIS)
FIELDS COVERED: Labour economics and sociology, vocational
training, etc. Economic and social development
TYPE OF SERVICE: Acts as international clearing house on
labour questions; developing information network with other
international organisations through OECD Development Centre
AVAILABILITY: Available to individuals on request to ILO
CHARGES: None at present
SIZE, AND TYPE OF FILES: Daily input of citations – 30;
daily output of citations – some 10–15 bibliographies (contain-
ing an average of 70 citations)
CURRENT SYSTEM: Computer-based

227 ORGANISATION: UNESCO
ADDRESS: Place de Fontenoy, 75 Paris 7ᵉ, France
TITLE OF SERVICE: Social Science Documentation Centre/Centre
de Documentation en Sciences sociales
FIELDS COVERED: Social and behavioural sciences, humanities
TYPE OF SERVICE: Inquiry service; selective dissemination;
publication
AVAILABILITY: Primarily to members of UNESCO and through
national commissions for UNESCO, to non-governmental
organisations, social science research, training and documentation
institutions and professional groups. Available to the public
through publications: (1) *World Index of Social Science
Institutions* (for details see under 'Sources'); (2) *Reports and
Papers in the Social Sciences* (English and French); (3) *Bibliography,
Documentation, Terminology* (English, French, Spanish and
Russian); (4) *International Social Science Journal* (English and
French)
LANGUAGE(S): English, French, Spanish
CHARGES: *Bibliography, Documentation, Terminology* – free to
professional institutions and interested scholars. Other
publications – varying
SIZE, AND TYPE OF FILES: Contacts with 1,800 institutions and
organisations, 1,700 social science specialists. Some 300

periodicals are scanned for material, and fugitive materials are received from all institutions with which the Centre is in touch. This is a continuing project of indefinite duration
CURRENT SYSTEM: Manual and computer based (OARE–UNESCO computerised data retrieval system for documentation in the social and human sciences)

228 ORGANISATION: United Nations Research Institute for Social Development
ADDRESS: Palais des Nations 1211, Genève 10, Switzerland
TITLE OF SERVICE: Data Bank of Development Indicators
FIELDS COVERED: Socio-economic data
TYPE OF SERVICE: Maintenance of data banks, in the first instance for the Institute's research
AVAILABILITY: Available to researchers
SIZE, AND TYPE OF FILES: Contains data on socio-economic indicators for 1960; updating in progress. Worldwide coverage
CURRENT SYSTEM: Machine-based. Items available in hard copy, on punched cards or tape

Ireland (Eire)/Irlande

229 ORGANISATION: The Economic and Social Research Institute (ESRI)
ADDRESS: 4 Burlington Road, Dublin 4
FIELDS COVERED: Social sciences relating to Ireland in particular
TYPE OF SERVICE: Library. Publication programme (including *Register of Research Projects in the Social Sciences in progress in Ireland*)
AVAILABILITY: To personnel, and to members of the public with authorisation
LANGUAGE(S): English, French
CHARGES: For photocopying
SIZE, AND TYPE OF FILES: Books, journals; card catalogues. Two staff
CURRENT SYSTEM: Manual

Italy/Italie

230 ORGANISATION: Centro internazionale bibliografico
ADDRESS: Palazzo Corsini, Via de Parione 11, 50123 Firenze
FIELDS COVERED: Bibliography and documentation
TYPE OF SERVICE: Bibliographies, photocopies, microfiches, reports
AVAILABILITY: General
LANGUAGE(S): Italian
CHARGES: On a fee-paying basis
SIZE, AND TYPE OF FILES: 312 periodicals, 20,626 abstracts, 35,000 descriptive fiches
CURRENT SYSTEM: Manual; own classification

Netherlands/Pays-Bas

231 ORGANISATION: Centrum voor Landbouwpublikaties en Landbouwdocumentatie
ADDRESS: Duivendaal 6a, Wageningen
FIELDS COVERED: Agriculture, economics, education, town and country planning, politics
TYPE OF SERVICE: Literature searches, SDI service
AVAILABILITY: General
LANGUAGE(S): Dutch, English
CHARGES: Dependent on subject of inquiry, time involved, etc. SDI: HF1·100 per year, plus HF1·1 per item.
CURRENT SYSTEM: UDC and special classification system of the Dokumentationsstelle Universität Hohenheim, Agrargeschichte und Dokumentationsstelle für Agrarpolitik, landwirtschaftliches Marktwesen und ländliche Soziologie, Bonn

232 ORGANISATION: Institute of Social Studies
ADDRESS: Molenstraat 27, 's Gravenhage
TITLE OF SERVICE: Library and documentation division
FIELDS COVERED: Social sciences, economics, sociology; emphasis on development
TYPE OF SERVICE: Referral service; review of documents in the library of the ISS; lists of new acquisitions; literature searches
AVAILABILITY: Publications available to interested institutes, universities and individuals; literature searches restricted to staff and participants

LANGUAGE(S): English
CHARGES: None
SIZE, AND TYPE OF FILES: Card index (geographical, alphabetical) containing books, documents and journal articles (abstracts) in the ISS library. 17,500 books, 400 periodicals, 15,000 documents. Nine library and documentation staff
CURRENT SYSTEM: Manual; cross-reference files

233 ORGANISATION: Sociaal-wetenschappelijk Informatie- en Documentatiecentrum (Koninklijke Nederlandse Akademie van Wetenschappen, Sociaal-wetenschappelijke Raad)
ADDRESS: Keizersgracht 569–571, Amsterdam
FIELDS COVERED: Social sciences. Information on current and finished empirical research in the social sciences in the Netherlands (most important part); social science literature in general; the structure of information resources in the social sciences in the Netherlands. The social science data archive of the Steinmetz Institute was taken over in 1972
TYPE OF SERVICE: Question answering; prefabricated and specially prepared bibliographies; inquiry service relating to data archive
AVAILABILITY: General
LANGUAGE(S): Dutch and English
CHARGES: None
CURRENT SYSTEM: Thesaurus (in preparation) will be mechanised. Data on punched cards

234 ORGANISATION: Steinmetz Stichting
ADDRESS: Herengracht 457, Amsterdam
FIELDS COVERED: Social sciences. Collects and makes retrievable the results of research in the field of social sciences, e.g. of post-1945 Gallup polls from all over the world
TYPE OF SERVICE: Data archive; inquiry service
AVAILABILITY: General
LANGUAGE(S): English
CHARGES: Restitution of material costs
SIZE, AND TYPE OF FILES: The collection consists of the results of about 250 surveys
CURRENT SYSTEM: Data on punched cards

NOTE: Now administered by Sociaal-wetenschappelijk Informatie- en Documentatiecentrum (see entry 233 above)

Norway/Norvège

235 ORGANISATION: Norsk Samfunsvitenskaplig Datatjenste
ADDRESS: Munthesgate 31, Oslo 2
FIELDS COVERED: All social sciences
TYPE OF SERVICE: (1) Information on data sets; (2) Data bank
for ecological sets 1945—70; (3) information on software for
social science analyses
AVAILABILITY: To members
LANGUAGE(S): Norwegian, English
CHARGES: Cost of transmission; publications free to members
SIZE: Oslo (Central Secretariat) — four staff; Bergen — one data
secretary; Trondheim — one data secretary
CURRENT SYSTEM: Data banks computerised; inventories partly
computerised

Sweden/Suède

236 ORGANISATION: Scandinavian Institute of African Studies
ADDRESS: Box 345, S751 06 Uppsala 1
FIELDS COVERED: Political science, economics, sociology, social
anthropology, modern history, economic history, popular
literature
TYPE OF SERVICE: Query answering, reference work, literature
searches, preparation of bibliographical materials, inter-library
loans
AVAILABILITY: General
LANGUAGE(S): Swedish, English, German, French
CHARGES: For photocopies and some published material
SIZE, AND TYPE OF FILES: Library with card catalogues.
17,000 volumes; 2,000 periodicals; union catalogue of Africana
in Nordic countries. Eight staff
CURRENT SYSTEM: Manual

237 ORGANISATION: Dokumentationsstelle für Fragen der
  Wissenschaftspolitik
  ADDRESS: Zentral- und Parlaments-Bibliothek, Bundeshaus,
  3003 Bern
  FIELDS COVERED: Planning and policy for scientific research
  TYPE OF SERVICE: Documentation for administration and
  direction of Swiss universities
  AVAILABILITY: Restricted at present to Swiss members of
  parliament and to the administration. May be extended to the
  Swiss universities and perhaps to a wider circle of users in future
  LANGUAGE(S): French and German
  CHARGES: All costs are met by the Confederation

238 ORGANISATION: Institut universitaire des hautes Études
  internationales, Genève
  ADDRESS: Rue de Lausanne 32, Genève
  TITLE OF SERVICE: (1) Library; (2) Centre for Documentation
  and Research on Asia (Centre de Documentation et de
  Recherche sur l'Asie)
  FIELDS COVERED: International relations, economics, social
  history
  TYPE OF SERVICE: Documentation services to students and
  staff registered with the Institute
  AVAILABILITY: Restricted, but access to card catalogues
  permitted to researchers
  LANGUAGE(S): French, English, Dutch, Russian
  CHARGES: Service charge for photocopying only
  SIZE, AND TYPE OF FILES: 80,000 books and 620 periodicals;
  depository library for UN publications; clippings (subscribes to
  Archives '69); microfiche of documents of the organisation of
  African States, documentation of international organisations, etc.
  Card indexes of stock, and of other collections. Staff regularly
  engaged in information activities
  CURRENT SYSTEM: Manual

239 ORGANISATION: African Studies Association of the United
     Kingdom
    ADDRESS: c/o Centre for West African Studies, University of
     Birmingham, PO Box 363, Birmingham B15 2SD
    FIELDS COVERED: Africa
    TYPE OF SERVICE: Query answering; referral
    AVAILABILITY: General
    LANGUAGE(S): English

240 ORGANISATION: Africa Studies Centre, University of Cambridge
    ADDRESS: Sidgwick Avenue, Cambridge
    FIELDS COVERED: Interdisciplinary research in modern African
     studies in the field of the social sciences
    TYPE OF SERVICE: Library and bibliographical service,
     accessions list, inquiries
    AVAILABILITY: Mainly for research staff and students
    LANGUAGE(S): English
    SIZE, AND TYPE OF FILES: Books, conference proceedings,
     unpublished material, ephemera, press-cuttings. Card
     catalogues. Two staff
    CURRENT SYSTEM: Manual

241 ORGANISATION: Aslib (Association of Special Libraries and
     Information Bureaux)
    ADDRESS: 3 Belgrave Square, London SW1
    FIELDS COVERED: Information science
    TYPE OF SERVICE: Intelligence services; register of translations,
     translators, indexers
    AVAILABILITY: Members
    LANGUAGE(S): English

242 ORGANISATION: Hispanic and Luso-Brazilian Council
    ADDRESS: Canning House, 2 Belgrave Square, London SW1
    TITLE OF SERVICE: Information Bureau
    FIELDS COVERED: Information on Spain, Portugal and Latin
     America
    TYPE OF SERVICE: Information bureau and library
    AVAILABILITY: General
    LANGUAGE(S): English, Spanish, Portuguese

CHARGES: None
SIZE, AND TYPE OF FILES: Library of 38,000 volumes, 300
    current periodicals

243 ORGANISATION: International African Institute
    ADDRESS: St Dunstan's Chambers, 10/11 Fetter Lane, Fleet St.,
      London EC1
    TITLE OF SERVICE: Information and Liaison Service
    FIELDS COVERED: Africa – social, cultural, linguistic
    TYPE OF SERVICE: Information and referral
    AVAILABILITY: General
    LANGUAGE(S): English

244 ORGANISATION: Local authority information department
    ADDRESS: Local authority (services are operated by most local
      authorities in the UK)
    FIELDS COVERED: Information, for citizens and visitors to the
      area, on local industrial, cultural, social and tourist matters
    TYPE OF SERVICE: Information service
    AVAILABILITY: General
    LANGUAGE(S): English

245 ORGANISATION: Polish Cultural Institute
    ADDRESS: 16 Devonshire Street, London W1
    FIELDS COVERED: Poland – science and culture
    TYPE OF INFORMATION: Documentation and information
    AVAILABILITY: General

246 ORGANISATION: University of London, Institute of Latin
      American Studies
    ADDRESS: 31 Tavistock Square, London WC1H 9HA
    FIELDS COVERED: All aspects of Latin America, from art and
      imaginative literature to original pure science
    TYPE OF SERVICE: Query answering using reference library of
      bibliographies and reference works, union catalogue, and
      knowledge of the field. Inquirers are referred, where appropriate,
      to other possible sources of information. Dissemination of *New
      Latin American Titles* to interested libraries
    AVAILABILITY: Due to staff limitations service may be
      restricted, with university work given first priority
    LANGUAGE(S): English, Spanish, French

CHARGES: None

SIZE, AND TYPE OF FILES: Approx. 2,000 volumes of books and periodicals. Card file with 70,000 entries covering works (including periodicals and Library of Congress purchases) relating to Latin America. Up-to-date lists of additions to the catalogue (*New Latin American Titles*). Growing file of machine-readable data for the preparation of cumulative author and subject indexes. Four staff

CURRENT SYSTEM: Mixture of manual and machine methods

247 ORGANISATION: Social Science Research Council

ADDRESS: State House, High Holborn, London WC1

FIELDS COVERED: Social sciences

TYPE OF SERVICE: Information on social science research. Publishes *SSRC Newsletter*

AVAILABILITY: General

LANGUAGE(S): English

CHARGES: None

248 ORGANISATION: United Nations Information Centre Library

ADDRESS: 14–15 Stratford Place, London W1

FIELDS COVERED: Comprehensive collection of UN documents and selected agency publications

TYPE OF SERVICE: Reference; Press Office; Visual Information Section

AVAILABILITY: General

249 ORGANISATION: United States Information Service (Reference Library)

ADDRESS: American Embassy, PO Box 214, Grosvenor Square, London W1

FIELDS COVERED: United States of America

TYPE OF SERVICE: US reference service for media representatives and government officials

250 ORGANISATION: University of Sussex, Institute of Development Studies

ADDRESS: University of Sussex, Falmer, Brighton

TITLE OF SERVICE: Institute of Development Studies Library

FIELDS COVERED: Economics, sociology, anthropology, politics, and international affairs in relation to overseas development

TYPE OF SERVICE: Query answering and reference work; inter-library loans service; literature searches; preparation of country and subject guides to development literature

AVAILABILITY: Letter of introduction required. Postgraduate researchers may borrow at the Librarian's discretion

LANGUAGE(S): Primarily English; correspondence in French, German and Spanish

CHARGES: For photocopying and for postage incurred in inter-library loans. Reciprocal exchanges are set up in preference to charging third-world countries for publications

SIZE, AND TYPE OF FILES: Official and non-official monographs and serials; international publications; microfilm and microfiche collections. At 1 January 1973, there were approx. 8,500 new serial titles on file (both official and non-official) and 42,000 books. Fourteen library staff (five spend part of their time in information activities)

CURRENT SYSTEM: Manual

Social Policy and Social Administration/ Politique Sociale et Administration Sociale

Belgium/Belgique

251 ORGANISATION: Association nationale pour la Prévention des Accidents du Travail/Nationale Vereniging tot Voorkoming van Arbeidsongevallen
ADDRESS: Rue de la Sablonnière 20, 1000 Bruxelles
FIELDS COVERED: Industrial and occupational safety
TYPE OF SERVICE: Query answering, reference work, bibliographical research
AVAILABILITY: Generally restricted to staff; to members of the public with authorisation
LANGUAGE(S): French, Flemish, English, German, Italian
CHARGES: For photocopying and for bibliographical work (various rates)
SIZE: Four staff
CURRENT SYSTEM: Manual

252 ORGANISATION: Association nationale d'Aide aux Handicapés mentaux (ANAHM)
ADDRESS: Rue Forestière 12, 1050 Bruxelles
FIELDS COVERED: Medicine, rehabilitation, education, accommodation, social services
TYPE OF SERVICE: Information and library service
AVAILABILITY: General
LANGUAGE(S): French, Flemish, English
CHARGES: For photocopying
SIZE, AND TYPE OF FILES: Card catalogues, periodicals. Four staff
CURRENT SYSTEM: Manual

253 ORGANISATION: Centre d'Études et de Documentation
sociales (CEDS)
ADDRESS: Rue Louvrex 47, 4000 Liège
FIELDS COVERED: Social affairs
TYPE OF SERVICE: Bibliographical research; information on
social legislation, etc.
AVAILABILITY: Mainly to students of affiliated schools and
members of CEDS
LANGUAGE(S): French
CHARGES: None
SIZE, AND TYPE OF FILES: Card catalogues; approx. 300
subscriptions to periodicals; edge-punched card system for
abstracts. Two staff
CURRENT SYSTEM: Mainly manual

254 ORGANISATION: Fonds d'Études pour la Sécurité Routière/
Fondsstudie voor Veilig Wegverkeer (FESR/FSVW)
ADDRESS: Rue du Gouvernement Provisoire 14, 1000 Bruxelles
FIELDS COVERED: All aspects of road safety, including
psychological and sociological aspects
TYPE OF SERVICE: Inquiries, reference work, bibliographical
research
AVAILABILITY: General
LANGUAGE(S): French, Flemish, English, German
CHARGES: For photocopying and translation
SIZE, AND TYPE OF FILES: Card catalogues; periodicals;
machine-readable files under consideration. Six staff
CURRENT SYSTEM: Manual, with likelihood of machine-based
services later

255 ORGANISATION: Geel Family Care Research Project,
Studiecentrum voor Gezinsverpleging (GRP)
ADDRESS: Passtraat 179, 2440 Geel
FIELDS COVERED: Psychology, sociology, social psychology,
history, anthropology
TYPE OF SERVICE: Query answering
AVAILABILITY: To members of the public with authorisation
LANGUAGE(S): Flemish, English
CHARGES: For reprographic work
SIZE, AND TYPE OF FILES: Card catalogues, periodicals. Two staff
CURRENT SYSTEM: Manual

256 ORGANISATION: Institut national du Logement
ADDRESS: Boulevard Saint-Lazare, 1030 Bruxelles
FIELDS COVERED: Housing, architecture, building techniques
and materials
TYPE OF SERVICE: Library; information service; publications
AVAILABILITY: General
LANGUAGE(S): Flemish and French

257 ORGANISATION: Ministère de l'Emploi et du Travail,
Administration de l'Hygiène et de la Médecine du Travail
ADDRESS: Rue Belliard 53, 1040 Bruxelles
FIELDS COVERED: Industrial medicine
TYPE OF SERVICE: Library; study service; publications;
information service (supply of photocopies, bibliographical
searches, etc.)
AVAILABILITY: General
LANGUAGE(S): Flemish, French, English, German
SIZE: Approx. 1,000 items. Six staff
CURRENT SYSTEM: Manual

258 ORGANISATION: Office national de Sécurité sociale (ONSS)
ADDRESS: Boulevard de Waterloo 76, 1000 Bruxelles
FIELDS COVERED: Current documentation relating to the social
sciences in general
TYPE OF SERVICE: Query answering, reference work, biblio-
graphical research
AVAILABILITY: To personnel, and to members of the public
with authorisation
LANGUAGE(S): French, Flemish
CHARGES: None
SIZE, AND TYPE OF FILES: Card catalogues (approx. 55,000
items); special collections of parliamentary documents; press
files. Eight staff
CURRENT SYSTEM: Manual

Canada

259 ORGANISATION: Canadian Council on Social Development/Le
Conseil canadien de Développement social
ADDRESS: 55 Parkdale, Ottawa K1Y 1E5, Ontario
FIELDS COVERED: Social services, social policy development,
social justice, social planning, criminology and corrections,
income security, housing
TYPE OF SERVICE: Specialised services of small professional
staff; query answering and referral activities. Publishes
Canadian Welfare, Bien-être social canadien, Social Development
(newsletter), *Housing and People* (newsletter), and directories of
welfare services. Issues reports and policy statements
AVAILABILITY: General
LANGUAGE(S): English, French
CHARGES: For publications
SIZE, AND TYPE OF FILES: Small specialised library. Staff
available as an information resource rather than as a formal
information service
CURRENT SYSTEM: Manual

France

260 ORGANISATION: Action populaire
ADDRESS: 15 rue Marcheron, Vanves
TITLE OF SERVICE: Centre de Documentation
FIELDS COVERED: Social policy, professional training, economics,
sociology, international relations, Communist ideology
TYPE OF SERVICE: Consultation on the spot; bibliography on
demand
AVAILABILITY: General
SIZE, AND TYPE OF FILES: 80,000 works; 1,200 periodicals
abstracted
CURRENT SYSTEM: Manual

261 ORGANISATION: Caisse nationale des Allocations familiales
(CNAF)
ADDRESS: 63 boulevard Haussmann, Paris 8^e
TITLE OF SERVICE: Centre de Documentation générale

FIELDS COVERED: Family and social policy (including their economic and cultural aspects)
TYPE OF SERVICE: Consultation on the spot; documentation service on demand
AVAILABILITY: General
CHARGES: none
SIZE, AND TYPE OF FILES: 5,000 works; 367 periodicals selectively abstracted
CURRENT SYSTEM: Manual

262 ORGANISATION: Institut national d'Études démographiques (INED)
ADDRESS: 27 rue du Commandeur, Paris 14^e
TITLE OF SERVICE: Centre de Documentation
FIELDS COVERED: Social sciences, demography, urbanism, labour, employment, social policy
TYPE OF SERVICE: Consultation on the spot; bibliography on demand
AVAILABILITY: General
SIZE, AND TYPE OF FILES: 20,000 works, 525 periodicals (about 100 directly concern social policy)
CURRENT SYSTEM: Manual

263 ORGANISATION: Institut national pour la Formation des Adultes (INFA)
ADDRESS: 18 rue des Tilleuls, 92 Boulogne-sur-Seine
TITLE OF SERVICE: Service d'Information et de Documentation sur la Formation des Adultes (SIDFA)
FIELDS COVERED: Further education (colloquia, congresses, training organisations). Study of techniques and methods of training
TYPE OF SERVICE: Query answering. Co-ordination of action in the field of further education
AVAILABILITY: General
CHARGES: None
SIZE, AND TYPE OF FILES: 1,500 research reports, 3,000 works (collection of course syllabuses, mostly Anglo-American), 250 periodicals
CURRENT SYSTEM: Manual

264 ORGANISATION: Service de Documentation de l'Équipe de
Sociologie du Loisir et des Modèles culturels (formerly Groupe de
Sociologie du Loisir et de la Culture populaire) CNRS, Paris
ADDRESS: 82 rue Cardinet, Paris 17ᵉ

FIELDS COVERED: Sociology of leisure – leave, holidays, tourism;
artistic and cultural leisure activities; sport; economics of leisure;
statistics; legislation. Documentation for France and various
other countries (especially USA, USSR, Czechoslovakia, Sweden,
Switzerland, Canada, Quebec, West Germany)

TYPE OF SERVICE: Information service; regular collaboration with
ongoing sociological research; documentary help and advice for
French and foreign students; indexes, bibliographies, abstracts,
etc.

AVAILABILITY: General, but priority given to researchers,
students and teachers

LANGUAGE(S): Various

CHARGES: None

SIZE, AND TYPE OF FILES: Approx. 6,000 works (articles, reports,
etc.), 800 dossiers, 60 reviews

CURRENT SYSTEM: Manual. Project in hand to co-ordinate
documentation gathered in Europe and North America, under the
auspices of the Comité du Recherche de Loisir et de la Culture
populaire de l'Association Internationale de Sociologie

Germany (Federal Republic)/République fédérale d'Allemagne

265 ORGANISATION: Institut für Arbeitsmarkt- und
Berufsforschung der Bundesanstalt für Arbeitsvermittlung und
Arbeitslosenversicherungen
ADDRESS: 8520 Erlangen, Strümpellstrasse 14
TITLE OF SERVICE: Forschungsdokumentation zur
Arbeitsmarkt- und Berufsforschung
FIELDS COVERED: Labour and professional markets
TYPE OF SERVICE: Query answering
AVAILABILITY: General
LANGUAGE(S): German
SIZE: 1,500 research projects
CURRENT SYSTEM: Computerised

International

266 ORGANISATION: Bureau international du Travail (BIT)
ADDRESS: Rue de Lausanne 154–156, Genève, Switzerland
TITLE OF SERVICE: Centre international de Sécurité (CIS)
FIELDS COVERED: Social security; occupational health
TYPE OF SERVICE: Information service
AVAILABILITY: General
LANGUAGE(S): French, English, German, Russian, Italian
CHARGES: Various
CURRENT SYSTEM: Manual; faceted classification

267 ORGANISATION: Council of Europe
ADDRESS: Avenue d l'Europe, 67 Strasbourg, France
TITLE OF SERVICE: Social Documentation Centre
FIELDS COVERED: Social policy, social legislation, social
problems, public health, housing, labour, etc.
TYPE OF SERVICE: Indexing of periodicals; compilation on
request of bibliographies of articles from periodicals on given
subjects. Bibliographical bulletin 18 times a year
AVAILABILITY: General
LANGUAGE(S): Various
CHARGES: None
SIZE, AND TYPE OF FILES: Card catalogue. 500 periodicals
indexed; approx. 5,000 new references added each year
CURRENT SYSTEM: UDC

United Kingdom/Royaume-Uni

268 ORGANISATION: Board for Information and National Tests in
Youth and Community Service
ADDRESS: 67 York Place, Edinburgh EH1 3JB
TITLE OF SERVICE: Scottish Youth and Community Information
Service
FIELDS COVERED: Youth and community work information
TYPE OF SERVICE: Information, bulletins, etc.
AVAILABILITY: General
LANGUAGE(S): English

269 ORGANISATION: Health Education Council
ADDRESS: Lynton House, 7–12 Tavistock Square, London WC1
FIELDS COVERED: Health education; advisory service with
information facilities
TYPE OF SERVICE: Information facilities
LANGUAGE(S): English

270 ORGANISATION: Medical Council on Alcoholism
ADDRESS: 74 New Oxford Street, London WC1
FIELDS COVERED: Alcoholism
TYPE OF SERVICE: Acquisition and dissemination of
information
AVAILABILITY: On inquiry
LANGUAGE(S): English

271 ORGANISATION: National Childrens Bureau
ADDRESS: Adam House, 1 Fitzroy Square, London W1P 5AH
TITLE OF SERVICE: Information service
FIELDS COVERED: Children
TYPE OF SERVICE: (1) Query answering by letter, telephone or
personal visit; (2) *Spotlight* information handbooks; (3)
Highlight handsheets on various topics
LANGUAGE(S): English
AVAILABILITY: To professional people (including students), both
members and non-members
CHARGES: None
SIZE, AND TYPE OF FILES: Library, reading lists, keyword index,
film index
CURRENT SYSTEM: Manual

272 ORGANISATION: National Council of Social Service (Incorporated)
ADDRESS: 26 Bedford Square, London WC1
FIELDS COVERED: Voluntary social welfare. Central
co-ordinating body
TYPE OF SERVICE: General information and query service on
voluntary and statutory social service
AVAILABILITY: General
LANGUAGE(S): English

273 ORGANISATION: National Old People's Welfare Council
ADDRESS: 26 Bedford Square, London WC1

FIELDS COVERED: Care of the elderly
TYPE OF SERVICE: Information and advice; referral
AVAILABILITY: General
LANGUAGE(S): English

274 ORGANISATION: National Poisons Information Service
ADDRESS: Royal Victoria Hospital, Belfast 12
FIELDS COVERED: Constituents and toxicity of poisons
AVAILABILITY: To doctors

NOTE: Similar services elsewhere in UK (e.g. at Cardiff Royal
Infirmary)

275 ORGANISATION: Social Work Advisory Service (SWAS)
ADDRESS: 26 Bloomsbury Way, London WC1A 2SR
FIELDS COVERED: Education, training and careers in social work
and allied fields
TYPE OF SERVICE:

(1) Provision of information and advice on education, training
and careers in social work in response to postal inquiries. Cannot
deal with telephone inquiries or casual callers
(2)   Personal consultations for potential social workers
(3)   Provision of literature
(4)   Provision of audio-visual aids

Facilities available in London, Edinburgh, and Castlerock
(Northern Ireland)
AVAILABILITY: General
LANGUAGE(S): English
CHARGES: For selected publications. Publications subscription
scheme

276 ORGANISATION: Youth Service Information Centre
ADDRESS: 37 Belvoir Street, Leicester LE1 6SH
FIELDS COVERED: Youth service in England and Wales
TYPE OF SERVICE: Collection and indexing of information;
dissemination by means of digest
AVAILABILITY: General
LANGUAGE(S): English
CURRENT SYSTEM: Manual

Sociology/Sociologie

Belgium/Belgique

277 ORGANISATION: Centre d'Étude des Travaux d'Infrastructure
    rurale (CETIR)
    ADDRESS: Faculté des Sciences agronomiques de l'État, 5800
    Gembloux
    FIELDS COVERED: Agronomy, rural affairs
    TYPE OF SERVICE: Inquiry
    AVAILABILITY: Mostly to personnel and students
    LANGUAGE(S): French
    CHARGES: For photocopying
    SIZE, AND TYPE OF FILES: Card catalogues (approx. 12,000 items),
    periodicals. Four part-time staff
    CURRENT SYSTEM: Manual

278 ORGANISATION: Centre national de Sociologie du Travail (CNST)
    ADDRESS: c/o Institut de Sociologie, avenue Jeanne 44, 1050
    Bruxelles
    FIELDS COVERED: Occupational sociology
    TYPE OF SERVICE: Documentation
    AVAILABILITY: To personnel, and to members of the public
    with authorisation
    LANGUAGE(S): French
    CHARGES: None
    SIZE, AND TYPE OF FILES: Card catalogues (approx. 3,000 entries)
    CURRENT SYSTEM: Manual

279 ORGANISATION: Centre national de Sociologie du Travail, Section
    Loisir et Culture modernes (CNST)
    ADDRESS: Avenue Jeanne 44, 1050 Bruxelles
    FIELDS COVERED: Sociology of knowledge; leisure; culture; the
    family; survey research
    TYPE OF SERVICE: No specialised services
    AVAILABILITY: To the public on application
    LANGUAGE(S): French
    TYPE OF FILES: Card catalogues

France

280 ORGANISATION: Institut français de Presse (IFP)
ADDRESS: 27 rue Saint-Guillaume, 75 Paris 7^e
TITLE OF SERVICE: Centre de Documentation
FIELDS COVERED: Social sciences — information problems.
  (For France, from the beginnings to the present day;
  for other countries, for the 20th century only)
TYPE OF SERVICE: Acquisition, conservation and communication
  of documents (including books, periodicals, bibliographies,
  press-cuttings, sound tapes, etc.); indexing and abstracting;
  preparation of catalogues; supplying of references (especially
  from the library of the Fondation nationale des Sciences
  politiques) on demand
AVAILABILITY: Specialist public
LANGUAGE(S): Various
SIZE, AND TYPE OF FILES: 100 works, 70 periodicals, 23 numbers
  of *Études de Presse*
CURRENT SYSTEM: Traditional

Germany (Federal Republic)/République fédérale d'Allemagne

281 ORGANISATION: Institut für Demoskopie Allensbach
ADDRESS: 7753 Allensbach am Bodensee
TITLE OF SERVICE: *Allensbacher Berichte* (weekly); *Allensbach
  Inter-Media Analysis* (annual); *Market Data and Media* (annual);
  Allensbach Book Survey (fortnightly)
FIELDS COVERED: Market and motivation research; consumer and
  industrial surveys; opinion research, media and communication
  research; surveys for legal evidence
TYPE OF SERVICE: Provides data from archives to social
  scientists on request
AVAILABILITY: Some material restricted
LANGUAGE(S): German, English, French
CHARGES: Various
SIZE, AND TYPE OF FILES: Archive of 2,000 reports (80,000
  questions over 26-year period); 3,000 books; code book,
  questionnaire and punched-card archive. Four information staff,
  in collaboration with other specialists
CURRENT SYSTEM: Machine-based. IBM 1130 and Control Data

282 ORGANISATION: Universität zu Köln, Zentralarchiv für
    Empirische Sozialforschung
  ADDRESS: 5 Köln 41, Bochumer Strasse 40
  TITLE OF SERVICE: (1) *Empirische Sozialforschung 19* . . ., an
    annual description of planned, ongoing and completed social
    research projects in the West of Germany, Austria and the
    German-speaking part of Switzerland; (2) List of archive holdings
  FIELDS COVERED: All subject areas of empirical social research
  TYPE OF SERVICE: (1) Edited answers from original question-
    naires (comprising between 15 and 21 questions); (2) Archive
    number, title of survey, author, year of survey
  AVAILABILITY: Book publication; no restriction
  LANGUAGE(S): German
  CHARGES: None
  SIZE, AND TYPE OF FILES: Approx. 600 surveys on different
    subjects (on punched cards, tapes and disks). 10 to 14 staff
    engaged in general information activities
  CURRENT SYSTEM: Machine-based

283 ORGANISATION: Internationale Union für die Erhaltung der
    natürlichen Hilfsquellen
  ADDRESS: Bonn, Adenauer Allee 214
  TITLE OF SERVICE: References of the International Council of
    Environmental Law
  FIELDS COVERED: Environmental law
  TYPE OF SERVICE: Query answering
  AVAILABILITY: Mainly to members of the organisation
  LANGUAGE(S): German, English
  CURRENT SYSTEM: Computerised

Italy/Italie

284 ORGANISATION: Centro di documentazione e di studi sull'
informazione (CESDI)
ADDRESS: Via Fabio Massimo 60, 00192 Roma
TITLE OF SERVICE: Servizio documentazione
FIELDS COVERED: Mass communications, cultural policy
TYPE OF SERVICE: Bibliographies, photocopies, translations
AVAILABILITY: General
LANGUAGE(S): Italian
CHARGES: On a fee-paying basis
SIZE, AND TYPE OF FILES: 5,000 books and documents; 100
subscriptions to specialist publications
CURRENT SYSTEM: Manual; own classification

285 ORGANISATION: Istituto ricerche applicate, documentazione e
studi (IRADES)
ADDRESS: Via Paisiello 6, 00198 Roma
TITLE OF SERVICE: Sezione documentazione e informazione
FIELDS COVERED: Sociology of religion
TYPE OF SERVICE: Bibliographies, abstracts, translations,
information service, photocopies, microfiches
AVAILABILITY: General
LANGUAGE(S): Italian
CHARGES: On a fee-paying basis
SIZE, AND TYPE OF FILES: 400 subscriptions at present
CURRENT SYSTEM: Mechanised; own classification

Netherlands/Pays-Bas

286 ORGANISATION: Institute of the Sciences of the Press
ADDRESS: Oude Turfmarkt 151, Amsterdam
FIELDS COVERED: Mass communication
TYPE OF SERVICE: Query answering service; subject
bibliographies
AVAILABILITY: General
LANGUAGE(S): Dutch, English
CHARGES: None
SIZE, AND TYPE OF FILES: Probably about 200–300 queries
per year. 1,200–1,400 titles in 1969

CURRENT SYSTEM: Titles on punched cards; abstracts grouped by subjects (special subject system developed by the Institute)

United Kingdom/Royaume-Uni

287 ORGANISATION: Institute of Race Relations
ADDRESS: 36 Jermyn Street, London SW1
FIELDS COVERED: Relations between racial groups
TYPE OF SERVICE: Information service
AVAILABILITY: General
LANGUAGE(S): English

Statistics/Statistiques

Belgium/Belgique

288 ORGANISATION: Center for Operations Research and
        Econometrics (CORE)
     ADDRESS: De Croylaan 54, 3030 Heverlee
     FIELDS COVERED: Mathematics, statistics, economics, operations
        research
     TYPE OF SERVICE: Reference work, bibliographical research
     AVAILABILITY: To personnel
     LANGUAGE(S): English
     SIZE, AND TYPE OF FILES: Card catalogues. Two staff
     CURRENT SYSTEM: Manual

289 ORGANISATION: Institut national de Statistique
     ADDRESS: Rue de Louvain 44, 1000 Bruxelles
     FIELDS COVERED: Economic and social statistics
     TYPE OF SERVICE: Extensive publishing programme of
        statistical documentation
     AVAILABILITY: General
     LANGUAGE(S): French, Flemish
     CHARGES: For photocopying, photographic work, and publications

Canada

290 ORGANISATION: Statistics Canada/Statistiques Canada, Information
        Division, Marketing Services Branch
     ADDRESS: Ottawa K1A 0T6, Ontario
     FIELDS COVERED: Census data; other statistical information
     TYPE OF SERVICE: Written and telephone inquiries handled;
        statistical information provided on request. Census data on
        computer summary tape and microfilm can be obtained from the
        User Enquiry Service, Census Branch, Statistics Canada, Ottawa
        K1A 0T5, Ontario
     AVAILABILITY: General

LANGUAGE(S): English and French
CHARGES: For publications, summary tapes and microfilm, and inquiries requiring special processing; none for general inquiries, etc.
TYPE OF FILES: Master computer files; printed publications; microforms
CURRENT SYSTEM: All statistical information processing is machine-based

Finland/Finlande

291 ORGANISATION: Central Statistical Office
ADDRESS: Annankatu 44, 00100 Helsinki
FIELDS COVERED: Government statistics, demography
TYPE OF SERVICE: Demand searches; computations from available primary data
AVAILABILITY: General — except for confidential primary data
LANGUAGE(S): Finnish, Swedish and English
CHARGES: On a fee-paying basis
CURRENT SYSTEM: Both manual and computerised

International

292 ORGANISATION: International Statistical Institute
ADDRESS: Oostduinlaan 2, 's Gravenhage, the Netherlands
FIELDS COVERED: Statistics
TYPE OF SERVICE: Mainly publications; query answering and referral service
LANGUAGE(S): English and French
CHARGES: In certain cases
TYPE OF FILES: Books and journals

Italy/Italie

293 ORGANISATION: Istituto centrale di statistica
ADDRESS: Via C. Balbo 16, Roma
TITLE OF SERVICE: Ufficio relazioni internazionale informazioni
FIELDS COVERED: Statistics
TYPE OF SERVICE: Bibliographical information service; treatment of statistical data
AVAILABILITY: General
LANGUAGE(S): Italian
CURRENT SYSTEM: Manual

Norway/Norvège

294 ORGANISATION: Statistisk Sentralbyrå (Central Bureau of Statistics of Norway)
ADDRESS: Droningensgate 16, Oslo-Dep, Oslo
FIELDS COVERED: Official statistics; social and economic studies
TYPE OF SERVICE: Information service concerning official statistics and analytical studies of social problems
AVAILABILITY: General (except for confidential primary data)
LANGUAGE(S): Norwegian and English
CHARGES: On a fee-paying basis; in some cases none
CURRENT SYSTEM: Computerised

United Kingdom/Royaume-Uni

295 ORGANISATION: The National Computing Centre Ltd.
ADDRESS: Quay House, Quay Street, Manchester 3
FIELDS COVERED: Computer usage, including Education Advisory Services, National Computer Program Index, etc.
TYPE OF SERVICE: Information service
AVAILABILITY: General
LANGUAGE(S): English
CHARGES: None

Information Sources/
Sources d'Information

Demography/Démographie

France

296 TITLE: *Guide de Recherches documentaires en Démographie*
PUBLISHING ORGANISATION: Institut national d'Études
démographiques (INED)
ADDRESS: Rue de la Sâone, Paris 14^e
FIELDS COVERED: Demography
TYPE OF INFORMATION: Statement of the problems posed by
demography and demographic documentation; characteristics,
methods and functions of demographic documentation
(bibliographical information)
AVAILABILITY: General
LANGUAGE(S): French
FREQUENCY: Published in 1966
PRICE: Fr. 40
CURRENT SYSTEM: Alphabetical author classification under
sub-headings; alphabetical subject catalogue; table of abstracted
annual statistics

297 TITLE: *Démographie: Tendances actuelles et Organisation de la
Recherche 1955–1965*
PUBLISHING ORGANISATION: Service d'Échange d'Information
scientifiques; Institut national d'Études démographiques
ADDRESS: 54 boulevard Raspail, 75 Paris 6e; 1 Rue de la Sâone,
75 Paris 14^e
FIELDS COVERED: Demography
TYPE OF INFORMATION: Part 1: analyses of works or articles
published in the last 10 years. Part 2: organisation of research;
documents and agencies that researchers can use; institutions and
manuals (dictionaries and bibliographies)
AVAILABILITY: General
LANGUAGE(S): French
FREQUENCY: Published in 1966
PRICE: Fr. 120

Economics/Économie

298 TITLE: *Bollettino d'informazione*
PUBLISHING ORGANISATION: Ministero del Bilancio e della
Programmazione economica
ADDRESS: Via XX Settembre, Roma
FIELDS COVERED: Economics, planning, social sciences
TYPE OF INFORMATION: (1) List of articles and publications;
(2) list of bodies and services in particular fields; (3) specialised
bibliographies
AVAILABILITY: General
LANGUAGE(S): Italian
FREQUENCY: Irregular, about twice a month
PRICE: Free
CURRENT SYSTEM: UDC classification

299 TITLE: *Documentazione di economia e politica agraria*
PUBLISHING ORGANISATION: Istituto di economia agraria
(INEA)
ADDRESS: Via Barberini 36, Roma
FIELDS COVERED: Economics, politics, agricultural sociology
TYPE OF INFORMATION: Abstracts of Italian and foreign
publications
AVAILABILITY: General
LANGUAGE(S): Italian
FREQUENCY: Irregular
CURRENT SYSTEM: Manual

300 TITLE: *Rassegna di letteratura sui cicli economici*
PUBLISHING ORGANISATION: Istituto nazionale per lo studio
della congiuntura (ISCO)
ADDRESS: Via Palermo 20, Roma
FIELDS COVERED: Economics
TYPE OF INFORMATION: Selected bibliography in economics
and statistics

AVAILABILITY: On demand
LANGUAGE(S): Italian
FREQUENCY: Three issues a year (from 1960)
PRICE: Free
SIZE: About 1,000 titles per issue

Education/Éducation

Germany (Federal Republic)/République fédérale d'Allemagne

301 TITLE: *Bibliographie moderner Fremdsprachenunterricht*
PUBLISHING ORGANISATION: Informationszentrum für Fremdsprachenforschung
ADDRESS: Marburg/Lahn, Liebigstrasse 37
FIELDS COVERED: Teaching of foreign languages
TYPE OF INFORMATION: Bibliography with abstracts
AVAILABILITY: General
LANGUAGE(S): German
FREQUENCY: Quarterly
PRICE: DM 40 per year
SIZE: 1,000 titles a year
CURRENT SYSTEM: Manual

302 TITLE: *Bibliographie Pädagogik*
PUBLISHING ORGANISATION: Pädagogisches Zentrum, Berlin
ADDRESS: Berlin 31, Berliner Strasse 40–41
FIELDS COVERED: Education
TYPE OF INFORMATION: Indexing
FREQUENCY: Bi-monthly
PRICE: DM 46 per year
SIZE: 400 journals scanned
CURRENT SYSTEM: Computerised

303 TITLE: *Bibliographie programmierter Unterricht*
PUBLISHING ORGANISATION: Pädagogisches Zentrum, Berlin
ADDRESS: Berlin 31, Berliner Strasse 40–41
FIELDS COVERED: Programmed instruction and educational technology
TYPE OF INFORMATION: Indexing
AVAILABILITY: On subscription
FREQUENCY: Bi-monthly
PRICE: DM 24 per year

SIZE: 120 journals scanned
CURRENT SYSTEM: Mechanised (paper tape); data structure
comparable with that of *Bibliographie Pädagogik* (see entry 302)

304 TITLE: *Dokumentation Jugendforschung, Jugendhilfe,
Jugendpolitik*
PUBLISHING ORGANISATION: Deutsches Jugendinstitut
ADDRESS: München 13, Infanteriestrasse 13
FIELDS COVERED: Youth education and sociology
TYPE OF INFORMATION: Abstracting service
AVAILABILITY: On subscription
LANGUAGE(S): German
FREQUENCY: Three issues a year
PRICE: DM 18 per year
SIZE: 900 entries a year
CURRENT SYSTEM: Manual

Italy/Italie

305 TITLE: *Quindicinale di note e commenti*
PUBLISHING ORGANISATION: Centro studi investimenti
sociali (CENSIS)
ADDRESS: Corso Vittorio Emanuele 251, 00186 Roma
FIELDS COVERED: Sociology of education and social policy
TYPE OF INFORMATION: In addition to other information on
current research projects conducted by the Centre, the review
publishes bi-monthly an 'Osservatorio dell'istruzione e delle
professioni', which consists mainly of statistical information
provided by original research
AVAILABILITY: General
LANGUAGE(S): Italian
FREQUENCY: Bi-monthly
PRICE: Annual subscription of Lire 15,000
SIZE: About 100 pages of statistical data
CURRENT SYSTEM: Own classification

Netherlands/Pays-Bas

306 TITLE: *Higher Education and Research in the Netherlands*
PUBLISHING ORGANISATION: Stichting der Nederlandse
Universiteiten en Hogescholen voor Internationale Samenwerking
(Netherlands Universities Foundation for International
Co-operation)
ADDRESS: Noordeinde Palace, Molenstraat 27, 's Gravenhage
FIELDS COVERED: Higher education
LANGUAGE(S): English, Spanish, French, German
FREQUENCY: Quarterly

United Kingdom/Royaume-Uni

307 TITLE: *Physical Education Yearbook*
PUBLISHING ORGANISATION: Physical Education Association of
Great Britain and Northern Ireland
ADDRESS: 10 Nottingham Place, London W1
FIELDS COVERED: Sport, physical education, recreation
TYPE OF INFORMATION: Information on research and develop-
ment trends; literature review; surveys; directory information
AVAILABILITY: General
LANGUAGE: English
FREQUENCY: Published annually
CURRENT SYSTEM: Manual

308 TITLE: *Yearbook of Educational and Instructional Technology,*
incorporating *Programmes in Print*
PUBLISHING ORGANISATION: Association for Programmed
Learning and Educational Technology
ADDRESS: 27 Torrington Square, London WC1
FIELDS COVERED: Programmed instruction courses, associated
equipment and teaching aids
TYPE OF INFORMATION: Classified listing with list of programme
users
AVAILABILITY: On subscription from Cornmarket Press Ltd.,
42 Conduit Street, London W1R 0NL
LANGUAGE(S): English
FREQUENCY: Published annually
PRICE £2.50
SIZE: Approx. 2,000 programmes listed

126

Environmental Planning/
Planification de l'Environnement

309 TITLE: *Dokumentation abgeschlossener und laufender Forschung auf dem Gebiet des Städtebaues, Wohnungs- und Siedlungswesens*
PUBLISHING ORGANISATION: Deutscher Verband für Wohnungswesen, Städtebau und Raumplanung e.V.
ADDRESS: Köln, Wrangelstrasse 12
FIELDS COVERED: Urban studies and town planning
TYPE OF INFORMATION: Abstracting service
AVAILABILITY: To all subscribers
LANGUAGE(S): German
FREQUENCY: Irregular
SIZE: 100 research projects
CURRENT SYSTEM: Manual

310 TITLE: *Dokumentation zur Raumordnung*
PUBLISHING ORGANISATION: Institut für Raumordnung
ADDRESS: 532 Bad Godesberg, Michaelshof
FIELDS COVERED: Country planning
TYPE OF INFORMATION: Comprehensive information on completed and current research projects
AVAILABILITY: Further details available from the above address
LANGUAGE(S): German
FREQUENCY: Continuous

Italy/Italie

311 TITLE OF PUBLICATION: *Tirés-à-part des Quaderni*
PUBLISHING ORGANISATION: Istituto di ricerca sulle acque del
Consiglio Nazionale delle Ricerche
ADDRESS: Via Reno 1, Roma
FIELDS COVERED: Water pollution, desalination, hydrology
TYPE OF INFORMATION: Bibliographies classified by UDC;
abstracts; articles
AVAILABILITY: SDI service in Italy. Available to foreigners
according to their interests
LANGUAGE(S): Italian, English, Esperanto
PRICE: Free
CURRENT SYSTEM: Peek-a-boo, UDC classification, thesaurus

Netherlands/Pays-Bas

312 TITLE: *Planning and Development in the Netherlands*
PUBLISHING ORGANISATION: Ministerie van Volkshuisvesting
en Ruimtelijke Ordening
ADDRESS: Noordeinde Palace, Molenstraat 27, 's Gravenhage
FIELDS COVERED: Environmental planning

Geography/Géographie

Germany (Federal Republic)/République fédérale d'Allemagne

313 TITLE: *Documentatio Geographica*
PUBLISHING ORGANISATION: Bundesforschungsanstalt für
Landeskunde und Raumordnung
ADDRESS: Bonn/Bad Godesberg, Michaelshof
FIELDS COVERED: Geography
TYPE OF INFORMATION: Indexing
AVAILABILITY: Subscribers
LANGUAGE(S): German
FREQUENCY: Bi-monthly
PRICE: DM 48 per year
SIZE: 400 journals scanned
CURRENT SYSTEM: Machine-based

Management

Germany (Federal Republic)/République fédérale d'Allemagne

314 TITLE: *Neue Betriebswirtschaft, Zeitschriften-Informationsdienst (ZID)*
   PUBLISHING ORGANISATION: Leitstelle Dokumentationsring
   Betriebswirtschaft
   ADDRESS: Frankfurt/Main, Gutleutstrasse 163–167
   FIELDS COVERED: Management, economics
   TYPE OF INFORMATION: Indexing
   AVAILABILITY: On subscription from Verlagsgesellschaft
   Neue Betriebswirtschaft, Heidelberg, Postfach 1920
   LANGUAGE(S): German
   FREQUENCY: Eight issues a year
   PRICE:DM 49 per year
   SIZE: 700 journals scanned; 2,500 entries a year
   CURRENT SYSTEM: Machine-based

Italy/Italie

315 TITLE: *L'Impresa*
   PUBLISHING ORGANISATION: FIUNIVER – Fondazione
   industria università division d'edition
   ADDRESS: Via Ventimiglia 115, 10126 Torino
   FIELDS COVERED: Management
   AVAILABILITY: Circulation 5,000
   LANGUAGE(S): Italian
   FREQUENCY: Two issues a year
   PRICE: Lire 9,000 per year

Political Science/ Sciences Politiques

Germany (Federal Republic)/République fédérale d'Allemagne

316 TITLE: *Politische Dokumentation*
PUBLISHING ORGANISATION: Leitstelle politische
Dokumentation
ADDRESS: Berlin 45, Paulinenstrasse 22
FIELDS COVERED: Political science, politics
TYPE OF INFORMATION: Abstracting service
AVAILABILITY: On subscription from Verlag Dokumentation,
München-Pullach, Kaiserstrasse 13
LANGUAGE(S): German
FREQUENCY: Monthly
PRICE: DM 180 per year
SIZE: 100 journals scanned; 1,800 abstracts a year
CURRENT SYSTEM: Manual

Italy/Italie

317 TITLE: *Problema della ricerca oggi in Italia*
PUBLISHING ORGANISATION: Laboratorio di studi sulla ricerca
e sulla documentazione
ADDRESS: Via Cesare de Lollis 12, Roma
FIELDS COVERED: Political science
AVAILABILITY: General
LANGUAGE(S): Italian
CURRENT SYSTEM: Manual

Psychology/Psychologie

France

318 TITLE: *Psychology—World List of Specialised Periodicals*
PUBLISHING ORGANISATION: Service d'Échange
d'Informations scientifiques (SEIS)/Maison des Sciences de
l'Homme
ADDRESS: 54 boulevard Raspail, 75 Paris 6^e
FIELDS COVERED: Psychology
TYPE OF INFORMATION: List of periodicals (with a detailed
descriptive note for each one) regularly publishing studies and
original articles, written by academics or specialists in the subject
AVAILABILITY: General
LANGUAGE(S): English and French
FREQUENCY: Published in 1967
PRICE: Fr. 38
SIZE: 106 subjects treated. Ten page index of titles; eight page index
of institutions
CURRENT SYSTEM: Alphabetical classification by country; index
of titles, of the institutions publishing the reviews, and of
subjects

Social and Behavioural Sciences/ Sciences Sociales et Sciences du Comportement

Austria/Autriche

319 TITLE: *Dokumentation und Information in Österreich —*
Dokumentationsführer für Wissenschaft, Technik und Wirtschaft
PUBLISHING ORGANISATION: Österreichische Gesellschaft für
Dokumentation und Bibliographie im Auftrag des
Bundesministeriums für Bauten und Technik
ADDRESS: A-1014 Wien, Josefsplatz 1
FIELDS COVERED: Science, technology, economics
TYPE OF INFORMATION: List of documentation centres in
Austria
AVAILABILITY: General
LANGUAGE(S): German
FREQUENCY: Only one edition published so far
PRICE: AS 70
SIZE: 1,000 pages

Canada

320 TITLE: *Inventory of Social Science Quantitative Data Sources in*
Canada
PUBLISHING ORGANISATION: Toronto Public Library
ADDRESS: College St./St George St., Toronto 28, Canada
FIELDS COVERED: Social sciences
TYPE OF INFORMATION: Description of characteristics of data
files, physical characteristics and status
AVAILABILITY: General
LANGUAGE(S): English and French
FREQUENCY: So far only one edition has been compiled (published
August 1971)
CURRENT SYSTEM: Manual

321 TITLE: *Bibliographies internationales spécialisées courantes francaises, ou à participation française*
PUBLISHING ORGANISATION: Direction des Bibliothèques de France (Commission nationale de Bibliographie)
ADDRESS: 58 rue de Richelieu, Paris
FIELDS COVERED: Social sciences (geography, cartography, history, sociology, ethno-anthropology, economics)
TYPE OF INFORMATION: Inventory of French specialist international bibliographies published at regular intervals
AVAILABILITY: General
LANGUAGE(S): French
FREQUENCY: Published in 1958
PRICE: Fr. 400
SIZE: 84 pages of references
CURRENT SYSTEM: Subject classification; within each category, listed by titles of periodicals. Subject index and index of titles of bibliographies and periodicals cited

322 TITLE: *Bulletin d'Information et de Liaison*
PUBLISHING ORGANISATION: Centre d'Études Africaines — CARDAN
ADDRESS: 20 rue de la Baume, Paris 8^e
FIELDS COVERED: Cultural aspects of Africa south of the Sahara; ethnography
TYPE OF INFORMATION: Inventory of African theses and research reports in the French language currently in preparation; French bibliography on Africa south of the Sahara; register of current African research in French; inventory of African theses and research reports maintained since 1966; inventory of African documentary resources in Paris
AVAILABILITY: General
LANGUAGE(S): French
FREQUENCY: Four volumes a year
PRICE: Fr. 70 per year
CURRENT SYSTEM: Manual; classification by country. Description, subject index, author index

323 TITLE: *Études africaines: Liste mondiale des périodiques spécialisés/African Studies: World List of Specialised Periodicals*

PUBLISHING ORGANISATION: Service d'Échange d'Informations scientifiques, Maison des Sciences de l'Homme, in collaboration with CARDAN

ADDRESS: 54 boulevard Raspail, 75 Paris 6^e

FIELDS COVERED: Social sciences

TYPE OF INFORMATION: List of periodicals dealing with Africa south of the Sahara:

A – Periodicals whose main concern is the study of Africa south of the Sahara

B – Social science periodicals for which this study is an important concern

C – Periodicals whose main concern is this study, but which are not scientific (providing information rather than research studies)

AVAILABILITY: General

LANGUAGE(S): French and English

FREQUENCY: Published in 1969

PRICE: Fr. 39

SIZE: 146 subjects dealt with for 50 countries. Index of institutions: 13 pages of names of institutions. Index of titles: 17 pages of titles

CURRENT SYSTEM: Alphabetical listing by country; geographical index, and index of titles, of institutions publishing reviews, and of subjects

324 TITLE: *Guides de Recherches*

PUBLISHING ORGANISATION: Fondation nationale des Sciences politiques

ADDRESS: 27 rue Saint-Guillaume, 75 Paris 7^e

FIELDS COVERED: Social sciences

TYPE OF INFORMATION: Each guide is dedicated to one section of research: study of French administration, study of contemporary Germany, study of China's problems, etc. Useful sources are presented for each of these in a systematic and selective manner and there is a bibliographical list of recently published works on the subject (classified by problem)

AVAILABILITY: General

LANGUAGE(S): French

FREQUENCY: Irregular (several issues a year)

PRICE: Variable
SIZE: Variable (several hundred references in each guide)
CURRENT SYSTEM: Systematic classification

325 TITLE: *Guide sommaire des Ouvrages de Référence en Sciences sociales*
PUBLISHING ORGANISATION: Fondation nationale des Sciences politiques
ADDRESS: 27 rue Saint-Guillaume, 75 Paris 7^e
FIELDS COVERED: Social sciences
TYPE OF INFORMATION: Selective and critical list of works of reference, bibliographies, specialised encyclopaedias, collections and indexes
AVAILABILITY: General
LANGUAGE(S): French
FREQUENCY: Irregular.

PRICE: Fr. 2·90 (1968 edition)
SIZE: 150 headings, 49 pages
CURRENT SYSTEM: Systematic list (by category) of works of reference. Alphabetical index of authors and titles

326 TITLE: *Périodiques spécialisés (Sciences de l'Homme)*
PUBLISHING ORGANISATION: Service d'Echange d'Informations scientifiques, Maison des Sciences de l'Homme
ADDRESS: 54 boulevard Raspail, 75 Paris 6^e
FIELDS COVERED: Social sciences
TYPE OF INFORMATION: Description of periodicals
AVAILABILITY: Specialised public
LANGUAG(ES): French
FREQUENCY: Fiche renewed each time a periodical starts, is modified, or stops publication
PRICE: 20 centimes per fiche for France and Europe; 25 centimes for others
SIZE: 4,000–4,200 fiches; 107 countries registered
CURRENT SYSTEM: Classification by country, and by alphabetical order within country

327 TITLE: *Dokumentation sozialwissenschaftlicher Forschung*
PUBLISHING ORGANISATION: Informationszentrum für
sozialwissenschaftliche Forschung
ADDRESS: Bonn/Bad Godesberg, Plittersdorfer Strasse 21
FIELDS COVERED: Social and behavioural sciences, economics,
education, political sciences, psychology
TYPE OF INFORMATION: List of the current research projects
of German-language social science institutes (for each project the
following information is provided: bibliographical data, key words
of contents, data for sociology of research); annual questionnaire
AVAILABILITY: General
LANGUAGE(S): German
FREQUENCY: Published annually
SIZE: 1,200–2,000 titles
CURRENT SYSTEM: Manual

328 TITLE: *Titelliste über Projekte sozialwissenschaftlicher Forschung*
PUBLISHING ORGANISATION: Koordinierungsstelle für die
Dokumentation sozialwissenschaftlicher Forschung
ADDRESS: 5 Köln-Lindenthal, Bochumer Strasse 40
FIELDS COVERED: Social sciences
TYPE OF INFORMATION: List of research projects by institution,
title of project, name(s) of researcher(s) – result of a questionnaire
sent out in 1968
LANGUAGE(S): German
FREQUENCY: Irregular
SIZE: Approx. 1,200 titles listed

329 TITLE: *Verzeichnis sozialwissenschaftlicher Forschungseinrichtungen
in der Bundesrepublik Deutschland*
PUBLISHING ORGANISATION: Verlag Otto Schwartz und Co.
ADDRESS: 34 Göttingen
FIELDS COVERED: Social sciences
TYPE OF INFORMATION: Catalogue of social science research
institutions in West Germany, with bibliographical supplement on
handbooks, dictionaries, bibliographies and periodicals
AVAILABILITY: General
LANGUAGE(S): German
FREQUENCY: Current edition published in 1966
SIZE: 100 pages (including 24 pages of supplement)

330 TITLE: *Abstracting Services vol. 2, 'Social sciences and humanities'*
PUBLISHING ORGANISATION: International Federation for
 Documentation
ADDRESS: Hofweg 7, 's Gravenhage, The Netherlands
FIELDS COVERED: Social sciences
TYPE OF INFORMATION: List of printed abstracting services:
 abstracting journals, selected primary journals with abstracts
 section, and card services
AVAILABILITY: General
LANGUAGE(S): English, French, Russian, Spanish
FREQUENCY: Irregular — first edition published in 1965, second
 in 1969. Currently updated in the monthly *FID News Bulletin*
PRICE: Hfl. 18 ($5)
SIZE: 92 pages
CURRENT SYSTEM: Alphabetical list of abstracting services; titles
 arranged by subject (according to UDC) and by country

331 TITLE: *Bibliography, Documentation, Terminology*
PUBLISHING ORGANISATION: UNESCO, Social Science
 Documentation Centre
ADDRESS: Place de Fontenoy, 75 Paris 7ᵉ, France
FIELDS COVERED: Social sciences
TYPE OF INFORMATION: (1) News of UNESCO; (2) bibliographical
 services throughout the world (covered by the manual *Les Services
 bibliographiques dans le Monde, 1960–1964*); (3) international
 and national activities
AVAILABILITY: General
LANGUAGE(S): English, French, Spanish, Russian
FREQUENCY: Bi-monthly
PRICE: Free to archives, libraries, documentation centres, and
 specialist institutions
SIZE: Variable
CURRENT SYSTEM: Divided into three large parts. Information
 relating to section (2) is classed, as soon as it reaches the Centre,
 according to the headings of the questionnaire reproduced at
 the end of the bulletin

332 TITLE: *Bibliographie des Répertoires mationaux de Périodiques en cours*
PUBLISHING ORGANISATION: UNESCO
ADDRESS: Place de Fontenoy, 75 Paris 7e, France
FIELDS COVERED: Social sciences
TYPE OF INFORMATION: List of national indexes of current periodicals. If none exists for a particular country, the most recent and complete multinational indexes are indicated. If there is no index for periodicals alone, current national bibliographies containing a section devoted to periodicals or articles from reviews publishing national bibliographies of periodicals, are shown
AVAILABILITY: General
LANGUAGE(S): French
FREQUENCY: Published in 1969
PRICE: Fr. 13
SIZE: 130 countries are examined
CURRENT SYSTEM: Alphabetically by country. A list of correspondents appears at the end of the volume

333 TITLE: *Confluence: Surveys of Research in the Social Sciences/ États des Recherches en Sciences sociales*
PUBLISHING ORGANISATION: Mouton and Co., for the Comité international pour la Documentation des Sciences sociales
ADDRESS: Mouton and Co. — PO Box 1132, 's Gravenhage, the Netherlands. Comité international pour la Documentation des Sciences sociales — 27 rue Saint-Guillaume, 75 Paris 7e, France
FIELDS COVERED: Social sciences
TYPE OF INFORMATION: Schedule of recent research and direction of current studies, accompanied by a selective bibliography on important problems of an interdisciplinary nature
AVAILABILITY: General
LANGUAGE(S): French or English (according to the volumes)
FREQUENCY: Irregular
PRICE: Variable
SIZE: Variable
CURRENT SYSTEM: Manual; systematic classification adapted to each subject and consequently varying with each volume

334 TITLE: *Index Bibliographicus vol. 2*
PUBLISHING ORGANISATION: International Federation for Documentation/Comité internationale pour la Documentation des Sciences sociales
ADDRESS: 27 rue Saint-Guillaume, 75 Paris 7e, France
FIELDS COVERED: Social sciences (except philosophy, history, humanities – but including economic and social history)
TYPE OF INFORMATION: List of analytical and bibliographical services permitting retrieval of articles and works from a definite branch of knowledge
AVAILABILITY: To libraries or institutions on demand
LANGUAGE(S): French
FREQUENCY: Published in 1964. No revision available (1974)
SIZE: 441 titles
CURRENT SYSTEM: UDC; index of subjects and titles cited

335 TITLE: *Inventaire des Organismes français actifs dans le Domaine du Développement*
PUBLISHING ORGANISATION: OECD
ADDRESS: 2 rue André Pascal, Paris 16e, France
FIELDS COVERED: Social sciences
TYPE OF INFORMATION: Notices on the French institutions of scientific and technical research that devote all or part of their activity to the study of the developing countries (address, organisation, methods of research, publications). Information on the institutions themselves and their activities in the way of documentation and publications (which often make them independent sources of information)
AVAILABILITY: General
LANGUAGE(S): French
FREQUENCY: Published in 1966
SIZE: 981 institutions on record
CURRENT SYSTEM: Organisations classified by activities and by country. List of main indexes that can be consulted, with complete titles. List of publications specialising in the problems of the developing countries

336 TITLE: *Reports and Papers in the Social Sciences* (series)
PUBLISHING ORGANISATION: UNESCO
ADDRESS: Place de Fontenoy, 75 Paris 7^e, France
FIELDS COVERED: Social sciences

TYPE OF INFORMATION: Directories, bibliographies, inventories, survey reports, studies on social science documentation
AVAILABILITY: General
LANGUAGE(S): English, French
FREQUENCY: Irregular. Two to three issues every two years
PRICE: Variable
SIZE: Quarto with a varying number of pages (50–250); the average size would be 100 pages
CURRENT SYSTEM: Varies with each number

337 TITLE: *Reports and Papers in the Social Sciences* no. 24, 'Guide pour l'établissement des centres nationaux de documentation en sciences sociales dans les pays en voie de développement'
PUBLISHING ORGANISATION: Comité international pour la Documentation des Sciences sociales; Maison des Sciences de l'Homme; UNESCO
ADDRESS: Place de Fontenoy, 75 Paris 7ᵉ, France
FIELDS COVERED: Social sciences
TYPE OF INFORMATION: List of the principal data on the problems of understanding and organisation that have to be posed and solved in order to set up a national documentation centre for the social sciences in a developing country; notably, a list of 'some works of reference'
AVAILABILITY: General
LANGUAGE(S): French and English
FREQUENCY: Published in 1969
PRICE: Fr. 24
SIZE: 92 works of reference cited
CURRENT SYSTEM: Six chapters, three annexes. The list of 'some works of reference' is annexe 1; the works are arranged alphabetically by type

338 TITLE: *Social Scientists Specialising in African Studies*
PUBLISHING ORGANISATION: UNESCO; École des hautes Études en Sciences sociales
ADDRESS: UNESCO – Place de Fontenoy. 75 Paris 7ᵉ, France; École des hautes Études en Sciences sociales, Centre d'Études africaines – CARDAN – 54 boulevard Raspail, 75 Paris 6ᵉ, France
FIELDS COVERED: Social sciences

TYPE OF INFORMATION: For each social scientist, biographical data such as the following are provided: name, scientific classification, nationality, birth date, university degrees, career, interests, present activity, membership of learned associations, publications, present postal address
AVAILABILITY: General
LANGUAGE(S): English, French
FREQUENCY: Present edition published 1963. No revision reported (1974)
PRICE: 1963 edition − £2·87½, $11·50, Fr. 40·00
SIZE: 1963 edition − 2,072 entries
CURRENT SYSTEM: Alphabetically arranged by name with a subject index at the end of the volume

339 TITLE: *World Index of Social Science Institutions*
PUBLISHING ORGANISATION: UNESCO, Social Science Documentation Centre
ADDRESS: Place de Fontenoy, 75 Paris 7^e, France
FIELDS COVERED: Social sciences
TYPE OF INFORMATION: List of social science research, advanced training, and documentation institutions and professional bodies
AVAILABILITY: General
LANGUAGE(S): English, French
FREQUENCY: The original publication (with ring binder) appeared in late 1970. A regular updating service is provided quarterly with every issue of the *International Social Science Journal*
PRICE: With ring binder − $15, £4·50, Fr. 60; without binder − $9, £2·70, Fr. 36. Annual subscription to the *International Social Science Journal* costs $7, £2·10, or Fr. 28
SIZE: Over 1,000 entries
CURRENT SYSTEM: Synoptic card indexing with supporting dossiers. The cards follow the pattern of the synoptic cards and are arranged alphabetically by country and by institution with the international ones coming first

340 TITLE: *World List of Social Science Periodicals*
PUBLISHING ORGANISATION: UNESCO, prepared by the International Committee for Social Science Information and Documentation

ADDRESS: UNESCO – Place de Fontenoy, 75 Paris 7^e, France;
ICSSID – 27 rue Saint-Guillaume, 75 Paris 7^e, France
FIELDS COVERED: Social sciences
TYPE OF INFORMATION: Detailed descriptive notices on
periodicals appearing all over the world and containing chiefly
original articles on one or other of the social sciences
AVAILABILITY: General
LANGUAGE(S): French and English
FREQUENCY: Irregular (first edition 1952, second 1956); since
the third edition, supplements have been published regularly,
three times a year, in the periodical *Social Science Information*
PRICE: Third edition – £3, $12, Fr. 41
SIZE: 1,350 entries, 448 pages. 1,320 periodicals analysed
CURRENT SYSTEM: Periodicals arranged alphabetically by
country. Countries arranged alphabetically according to their
French names, with their English names following. General index
of titles, and indexes of institutions and subjects, in both French
and English

Ireland (Eire)/Irlande

341 TITLE: *Register of Research Projects in the Social Sciences in
Progress in Ireland*
PUBLISHING ORGANISATION: The Economic and Social
Research Institute (ESRI)
ADDRESS: 4 Burlington Road, Dublin 4
FIELDS COVERED: Social sciences, for both Northern Ireland
and Eire
TYPE OF INFORMATION: Details of: (1) institution and research
worker; (2) subject; (3) existing reports; (4) expected date of
completion; (5) source of support
AVAILABILITY: General
LANGUAGE(S): English
FREQUENCY: Published semi-annually
PRICE: £0.25
SIZE: 14 pages; about 120 projects described

342 TITLE: *Istituti di studi e ricerche economiche, sociali e politiche*
PUBLISHING ORGANISATION: Centro di documentazione e di studi sull'informazione (CESDI)
ADDRESS: Via Fabio Massimo 60, Roma
FIELDS COVERED: Social science, economics, politics
TYPE OF INFORMATION: Details about the composition and activities of over 100 Italian research institutions and centres
AVAILABILITY: General
LANGUAGE(S): Italian
FREQUENCY: Published as an extract from *Annuario dell'economia della politica della cultura*, 1969
SIZE: 114 institutions detailed; 55 pages

343 TITLE: *Ricerche promesse dal CNR*
PUBLISHING ORGANISATION: Consiglio nazionale delle ricerche, Servizio sviluppo
ADDRESS: Piazzale delle Scienze 7, Roma
FIELDS COVERED: Social and behavioural sciences
TYPE OF INFORMATION: List of research financed by CNR in all fields
AVAILABILITY: General
LANGUAGE(S): Italian
FREQUENCY: Annually from 1967
CURRENT SYSTEM: Machine-based; KWIC indexes

344 TITLE: *Ricerche sociali in Italia (1945–1965),* compiled by T. Tentori
PUBLISHING ORGANISATION: Edizioni AAI
FIELDS COVERED: Social sciences
TYPE OF INFORMATION: Full information on duration, finance, methodology and results of research projects
AVAILABILITY: General
LANGUAGE(S): Italian
FREQUENCY: Supplements continue to appear regularly in the review *Assistenza d'oggi*

345 TITLE: *Scienze sociali. Bollettino d'informazione sull'organizzazione della ricerca e dell'insegnamento*
PUBLISHING ORGANISATION: Comitato per le scienze politiche e sociali (COSPOS)

ADDRESS: Viale Mazzini 88, Roma
FIELDS COVERED: Social sciences
TYPE OF INFORMATION: Information about the organisation of
  research and higher education – research in progress, research
  centres, conferences
AVAILABILITY: General
LANGUAGE(S): Italian
FREQUENCY: Irregular
PRICE: First two parts distributed free. Annual subscription (from
  the first number) Lire 4,000
SIZE: Contains information on some 20 research projects in
  progress, 3–4 research centres, and the proceedings of 5–6
  conferences

Netherlands/Pays-Bas

346 TITLE: *Bibliografie Sociaal-wetenschappelijk Onderzoek*
  PUBLISHING ORGANISATION: Koninklijke Nederlandse
    Akademie van Wetenschappen, Sociaal-wetenschappelijke Raad
  ADDRESS: Keizersgracht 569–571, Amsterdam
  FIELDS COVERED: Social and behavioural sciences
  TYPE OF INFORMATION: Bibliographical references to research
    reports that are not published as books or in journals and so are
    not easy to acquire. Information is given about whether a report
    is available and, if so, from where. Note: a great many (about
    700) of the reports mentioned in this bibliography are stored in
    the Rapportencentrale (clearing-house for reports in the social
    sciences) of the Sociaal-wetenschappelijke Raad, which started in
    1969
  AVAILABILITY: General
  LANGUAGE(S): Dutch
  FREQUENCY: Appears twice a year
  PRICE: Hfl. 14
  SIZE: Approx. 300 entries per volume
  CURRENT SYSTEM: Entries grouped by subject; subject indexes

347 TITLE: *Boletín de estudios latinoamericanos en Europa* (before
    1971, entitled *Boletín informativo*)
  PUBLISHING ORGANISATION: Studie- en Documentatiecentrum
    Latijns Amerika

ADDRESS: Mauritskade 63, Amsterdam
FIELDS COVERED: Political science, anthropology, economics,
sociology in relation to Latin America
TYPE OF INFORMATION: Lists of European research projects
concerned with Latin America
AVAILABILITY: Restricted to libraries and documentation
centres in Europe and America (North and South)
LANGUAGE(S): Spanish and English
FREQUENCY: Appears twice a year
PRICE: Free
SIZE: Approx. 40–50 entries per year
CURRENT SYSTEM: Entries grouped by discipline

348 TITLE: *Directorio de latinoamericanistas europeas/Directory of
European Latinamericanists*
PUBLISHING ORGANISATION: Studie- en documentatiecentrum
Latijns Amerika; Centre for Latin American Studies, St Anthony's
College, Oxford
ADDRESS: Mauritskade 63, Amsterdam; University of Oxford,
Oxford, England
FIELDS COVERED: Political science, anthropology, economics,
sociology, social geography in relation to Latin America
TYPE OF INFORMATION: List of researchers on Latin America;
their fields, publications, *curriculum vitae*, recent fieldwork
AVAILABILITY: Restricted (to libraries, institutions, field-workers,
etc.)
LANGUAGE(S): Spanish
FREQUENCY: First published in 1969. Extensions and corrections
published as an appendix to the *Boletín de estuadios latino-
americanos en Europa* (two issues a year)
PRICE: Free
SIZE: Approx. 150 entries
CURRENT SYSTEM: Regional; authors listed alphabetically

349 TITLE: *Informatie omtrent lopend Onderzoek in de Sociale
Wetenschappen*
PUBLISHING ORGANISATION: Koninklijke Nederlandse
Akademie van Wetenschappen, Sociaal-wetenschappelijke Raad
ADDRESS: Keizersgracht 569–571, Amsterdam
FIELDS COVERED: Social and behavioural sciences

TYPE OF INFORMATION: List of new research projects, changes in
current research projects, subjects of research that have been
stopped, addresses of organisations or persons in charge of the
research
AVAILABILITY: General
LANGUAGE(S): Dutch
FREQUENCY OF PUBLICATION: Two or three times a year
PRICE: Hfl. 7·50
SIZE: Approx. 350 entries
CURRENT SYSTEM: Entries are grouped in broad subjects

350 TITLE: *Register van lopend Onderzoek in de Sociale
Wetenschappen*
PUBLISHING ORGANISATION: Koninklijke Nederlandse
Akademie van Wetenschappen, Sociaal-wetenschappelijke Raad
ADDRESS: Keizersgracht 569–571, Amsterdam
FIELDS COVERED: Social and behavioural sciences (current
research projects in the Netherlands)
TYPE OF INFORMATION: List of current projects. Information
given includes: title of the project; a description of it; ways and
means; particulars concerning methods and theory; duration;
method of reporting; originator of the project; financing;
institute or person(s) carrying out the research
AVAILABILITY: To subscribers
LANGUAGE(S): Dutch, with annotations and indexes in English
FREQUENCY: Appears once a year
PRICE: Hfl. 25
SIZE: Over 1,000 entries (1967–68)
CURRENT SYSTEM: Entries classified by subject; geographical
classification of regional and local research projects

351 TITLE: *Wegwijzer*
PUBLISHING ORGANISATION: Koninklijke Nederlandse
Akademie van Wetenschappen, Sociaal-wetenschappelijke Raad
ADDRESS: Keizersgracht 569–571, Amsterdam
FIELDS COVERED: Social and behavioural sciences, including law
and history
TYPE OF INFORMATION: List of information and documentation
centres, libraries and archives; information on collections,
catalogues, activities, etc.
AVAILABILITY: General

LANGUAGE(S): Dutch
FREQUENCY: Published for the first time in 1971
PRICE: Hfl. 40
SIZE: Approx. 450 entries
CURRENT SYSTEM: Entries are grouped by city, them alphabetically; subject index

United Kingdom/Royaume-Uni

352 TITLE: *Aslib Directory vol. 2, 'Information sources in medicine, the social sciences and the humanities'*
PUBLISHING ORGANISATION: Aslib
ADDRESS: 3 Belgrave Square, London SW1
FIELDS COVERED: Includes social sciences
TYPE OF INFORMATION: Directory. Indicates the scope and publications of the information source in question
AVAILABILITY: General
LANGUAGE(S): English
FREQUENCY: Irregular
PRICE: £9·00 (£7·50 to members of Aslib)
SIZE: Approx. 2,750 sources
CURRENT SYSTEM: Manual

353 TITLE: *Directory of British Associations*
PUBLISHING ORGANISATION: CBD Research Ltd.
ADDRESS: 154 High Street, Beckenham, Kent
FIELDS COVERED: Associations of all kinds
TYPE OF SERVICE: Directory
AVAILABILITY: General
LANGUAGE(S): English
FREQUENCY: Published annually

354 TITLE: *Libraries, Museums and Art Galleries Yearbook*
PUBLISHING ORGANISATION: James Clarke & Co. Ltd. (London) and R.R. Bowker (New York)
ADDRESS: 7 All Saints Passage, Cambridge
FIELDS COVERED: Includes social sciences
TYPE OF SERVICE: Directory
AVAILABILITY: General
LANGUAGE(S): English

FREQUENCY: Irregular
PRICE: £4·75
SIZE: Approx. 2,500 entries
CURRENT SYSTEM: Manual

355 TITLE: *Library resources in . . .* (various volumes covering some
   regions of the British Isles)
   PUBLISHING ORGANISATION: Library Association, Reference,
   Special and Information Section
   ADDRESS: 7 Ridgmount Street, London WC1 7AE
   FIELDS COVERED: Includes social sciences
   TYPE OF INFORMATION: Directory. Gives information about
   holdings, coverage, availability, addresses, etc.
   AVAILABILITY: General
   LANGUAGE(S): English
   FREQUENCY: Irregular
   CURRENT SYSTEM: Manual

356 TITLE: *Scientific Research in British Universities and Colleges,
   vol. 3*
   PUBLISHING ORGANISATION: HMSO
   ADDRESS: Atlantic House, Holborn Viaduct, London EC1
   FIELDS COVERED: Social sciences
   TYPE OF INFORMATION: Register of research projects in
   progress
   AVAILABILITY: General
   LANGUAGE(S): English
   FREQUENCY: Published annually

357 TITLE: *World of Learning*
   PUBLISHING ORGANISATION: Europa Publications Ltd.
   ADDRESS: 18 Bedford Square, London WC1B 3JN
   FIELDS COVERED: Social sciences included
   TYPE OF INFORMATION: Directory. Material on institutions,
   publications
   AVAILABILITY: General
   LANGUAGE(S): English
   FREQUENCY: Published annually
   PRICE: £10·50
   CURRENT SYSTEM: Manual

Social Policy and Social Administration/ Politique Sociale et Administration Sociale

Austria/Autriche

358 TITLE: *KDZ – Literatur Rundschau*
PUBLISHING ORGANISATION: Kommunalwissenschaftliches Dokumentationszentrum (KDZ)
ADDRESS: A-1144 Wien, Linzerstrasse 452
FIELDS COVERED: Public finance, economics, administration, community affairs, environmental planning
TYPE OF INFORMATION: List of recently published literature, with abstracts
AVAILABILITY: General
LANGUAGE(S): German
FREQUENCY: Four issues a year

Germany (Federal Republic)/République fédérale d'Allemagne

359 TITLE: *Dokumentation Sozialmedizin, öffentlicher Gesundheitsdienst und Arbeitsmedizin*
PUBLISHING ORGANISATION: Institut für Dokumentation und Information über Sozialmedizin und öffentliches Gesundheits-wesen
ADDRESS: Bielefeld, Westerfeldstrasse 15
FIELDS COVERED: Social medicine, public health
TYPE OF INFORMATION: Abstracting, with annual index
AVAILABILITY: To subscribers
LANGUAGE(S): German
FREQUENCY: Monthly
PRICE: DM 30 per year

SIZE: 400 journals scanned; 1,500 entries a year
CURRENT SYSTEM: Manual

360 TITLE: *Informationsdienst Krankenhauswesen*
PUBLISHING ORGANISATION: Deutsches Krankenhausinstitut
ADDRESS: Düsseldorf, Tersteegenstrasse 9
FIELDS COVERED: Public health, hospital organisation
TYPE OF INFORMATION: Indexing
AVAILABILITY: On subscription from the Institut für
   Krankenhausbau der Techn. Universität Berlin, Berlin 12, Strasse
   des 17. Juni, 135
LANGUAGE(S): German
FREQUENCY: Quarterly
PRICE: DM 85 per year
SIZE: 235 journals scanned; 3,750 entries a year
CURRENT SYSTEM: Computerised

361 TITLE: *Sport-Dokumentation*
PUBLISHING ORGANISATION: Bundesinstitut für
   Sportwissenschaft
ADDRESS: Lövenich, Hertzstrasse 1
FIELDS COVERED: Part A — sport; Part B — sport medicine
TYPE OF INFORMATION: Abstracting service
AVAILABILITY: To subscribers
LANGUAGE(S): German
FREQUENCY: Monthly
PRICE: DM 72 per year
SIZE: Part A — 400 journals scanned; Part B — 800 journals scanned
CURRENT SYSTEM: Manual

362 TITLE: *Répertoire des Organismes d'Étude et de Recherche dans le Domaine culturel* (Sous la responsabilité de Claire Guinchat)
PUBLISHING ORGANISATION: Council of Europe
ADDRESS: Avenue de l'Europe, 67 Strasbourg, France
FIELDS COVERED: Leisure, culture, sport, cultural stimulation, tourism. The countries covered at present are Belgium, Cyprus, France, Great Britain, Italy and Sweden; work on Germany (Federal Republic) is in progress
TYPE OF INFORMATION: Name and address of each organisation; type of institution (public and private); name of director; branches of research
AVAILABILITY: General – on demand
LANGUAGE(S): English and French
FREQUENCY: Published in 1970
PRICE: Free
SIZE: Varies with each country
CURRENT SYSTEM: Manual

Sociology/Sociologie

Germany (Federal Republic)/République fédérale d'Allemagne

363 TITLE: *Dokumentation für Presse, Rundfunk und Film*
PUBLISHING ORGANISATION: Zeitungs- und
Zeitschriften-Verlag
ADDRESS: Bad Godesberg, Wurzerstrasse 46
FIELDS COVERED: Newspapers, broadcasting, film, mass
communication
TYPE OF INFORMATION: Bibliography
AVAILABILITY: To all subscribers
LANGUAGE(S): German
FREQUENCY: Quarterly
SIZE: 100 journals scanned
CURRENT SYSTEM: Manual

364 TITLE: *Entwicklungsländer-Studien*
PUBLISHING ORGANISATION: Deutsche Stiftung für
Entwicklungsländer
ADDRESS: Bonn, Blücherstrasse 16
FIELDS COVERED: All aspects of the social sciences in developing
countries
TYPE OF INFORMATION: Indexing
AVAILABILITY: To subscribers
LANGUAGE(S): German
FREQUENCY: Regular
CURRENT SYSTEM: Manual

365 TITLE: *Karlsruher juristische Bibliographie*
PUBLISHING ORGANISATION: C.H. Beck Verlag
ADDRESS: München 23, Wilhelmstrasse 9
FIELDS COVERED: Law
TYPE OF INFORMATION: Indexing
AVAILABILITY: To subscribers
LANGUAGE(S): German
FREQUENCY: Monthly

PRICE: DM 144 per year
SIZE: 650 journals scanned; 20,000 entries a year
CURRENT SYSTEM: Manual

366 TITLE: *Publizistikwissenschaftlicher Referatendienst*
PUBLISHING ORGANISATION: Institut für Publizistik der Freien
Universität Berlin
ADDRESS: Berlin 33, Hagenstrasse 56 ⅰ
FIELDS COVERED: Mass communication, film
TYPE OF INFORMATION: Abstracting service
AVAILABILITY: On subscription from Verlag Dokumentation,
8023 München-Pullach, Kaiserstrasse 13
LANGUAGE(S): German
FREQUENCY: Quarterly
PRICE: DM 68 per year
SIZE: 95 journals scanned; 3,260 abstracts a year
CURRENT SYSTEM: Manual; every edition has an author, keyword,
geographical and systematic index

International

367 TITLE: *Current Sociology/La Sociologie contemporaine*
PUBLISHING ORGANISATION: Mouton and Co., for
the Association internationale de Sociologie
ADDRESS: Mouton and Co. – PO Box 1132, 's Gravenhage, the
Netherlands. Association internationale de Sociologie – Via
Daverio 7, Milano 20122, Italy
FIELDS COVERED: Sociology
TYPE OF INFORMATION: 'Trend reports' accompanied by a
selective bibliography on the principal areas and problems of
sociology
AVAILABILITY: General
LANGUAGE(S): French, English
FREQUENCY: Three issues a year
PRICE: $9 per year
SIZE: From 400 to 800 references in each issue
CURRENT SYSTEM: Manual; systematic classification
adapted to each subject and consequently varying with each
volume

368 TITLE: *Bollettino bibliografico di informatica generale e applicata al diritto*
PUBLISHING ORGANISATION: Istituto per la documentazione giuridica del Consiglio Nazionale delle Ricerche
ADDRESS: Via Panciatichi 56/16, 50127 Firenze
FIELDS COVERED: Law, sociology of law
TYPE OF INFORMATION: Catalogue of works belonging to the institute library and dealing with the applications of computing to law
AVAILABILITY: General
LANGUAGE(S): English, French, Italian
FREQUENCY: Three issues a year
CURRENT SYSTEM: Computer-based; KWIC index

369 TITLE: *Industria culturale 1968*
PUBLISHING ORGANISATION: Centro di documentazione e di studi sull'informazione (CESDI)
ADDRESS: Via Fabio Massimo 60, Roma
FIELDS COVERED: Italian press and publishing
TYPE OF INFORMATION: Details of Italian daily newspapers, periodicals and reviews; details of publishers; short note on the state of publishing in Italy in 1967 and 1968; statistical break-down of book production, 1967–1968; bibliography on the structure and contents of the press (13 pages)
AVAILABILITY: General
LANGUAGE(S): Italian
FREQUENCY: Published as an extract from *Annuario dell'economia della politica della cultura,* 1969
SIZE: 105 pages

Information Research/
Recherche en Matière
d'Information

Criminology/Criminologie

Austria/Autriche

370 TITLE OF PROJECT: Stufenweise Entwicklung eines
   elektronischen Polizeiinformationssystems
   DESCRIPTION: Development of an electronic information system
   for police matters, especially criminal statistics
   NAME(S) OF RESEARCHER(S): Project leaders – Dr Lauscha,
   Dr Ambrosi
   ORGANISATION: Bundesministerium für Inneres
   ADDRESS: A-1014 Wien, Herrengasse 7
   RESEARCH METHODOLOGY: Computer-aided information system

Economics/Économie

Austria/Autriche

371 TITLE OF PROJECT: Wirtschaftsstatistische Datenbank
DESCRIPTION: Computer-aided documentation of economic
  data and statistics
NAME(S) OF RESEARCHER(S): Dr Wang
ORGANISATION: Österreichisches Institut für
  Wirtschaftsforschung
ADDRESS: A-1030 Wien, Arsenal
DURATION OF PROJECT: About one year, beginning in 1972

372 TITLE OF PROJECT: Wirtschaftspolitische Dokumentation
DESCRIPTION: Computer-aided documentation of literature and
  data in the field of economic policy
NAME(S) OF RESEARCHER(S): Dr Festa
ORGANISATION: Bundeskammer der gewerblichen Wirtschaft
ADDRESS: A-1010 Wien, Stubenring 12
DURATION OF PROJECT: Completed
LANGUAGE(S): German

France

373 TITLE OF PROJECT: L'information économique en France:
  le problème des Banques d'information
DESCRIPTION: Theoretical, political and practical analysis of the
  constitution of information banks. Exposé of a concrete
  example: the SPLEEN system in the economics of energy
NAME(S) OF RESEARCHER(S): Elisabeth Allaire
ORGANISATION: Centre de Documentation Sciences humaines du
  CNRS
ADDRESS: 54 boulevard Raspail, Paris 7^e
DURATION OF PROJECT: Completed
LANGUAGE(S): French

160

374 TITLE OF PROJECT: Préparation et expérimentation d'un
thésaurus pour le traitement de l'information en sciences
économiques
DESCRIPTION: Establishment of a structured bilingual vocabulary
(French–English) of the terms required to describe the contents
of economics documents, and for research, through classifying
the information contained in these documents. Experimental
application to the preparation of some indexes and
bibliographies
NAME(S) OF RESEARCHER(S): Jean Meyriat and Jean Viet
(directors of the project)
ORGANISATION: Comité international pour la Documentation
des Sciences sociales
ADDRESS: 27 rue Saint-Guillaume, 75 Paris 7^e
DURATION OF PROJECT: Preliminary version of the thesaurus
completed at the beginning of 1970; second version to be
completed in June 1971; experimentation in 1971 and 1972
SOURCE OF FINANCE: Originally from the reserve funds of the
Comité. Subsidies have been requested but not yet obtained
RESEARCH METHODOLOGY: Comparison of existing
vocabularies and lexicons, analysis of the indexes of specialist
bibliographies, analysis of primary documents
PUBLICATION: The thesaurus is intended for publication on
completion
LANGUAGE(S): English and French

Italy/Italie

375 TITLE OF PROJECT: Bibliografia sui modelli previsionali di
lungo periodo
DESCRIPTION: Bibliography on long-term forecasting, comprising
about 2,500 citations with a subject index of 13,000 subject and
6,000–7,000 subsidiary subject terms. Classification and indexing
NAME(S) OF RESEARCHER(S): Dott. Michelangelo Toglia,
Dott. Giguarella, Mme Margiotta
ORGANISATION: Istituto nazionale per lo studio della
congiuntura (ISCO)
ADDRESS: Via Milano 20, Roma
DURATION OF PROJECT: 1970–71

SOURCE AND SCALE OF FINANCE: 4 million lire a year from the Minstero del bilancio e della programmazione economica
PUBLICATIONS: Technical reports to funding body
LANGUAGE(S): Italian

376 TITLE OF PROJECT: L'attività di documentazione economica nella P.A. e in altri istituti
DESCRIPTION: To see whether, and by what methods, economic documentation has been collected, conserved and disseminated. One part of the research concerned university institutes of economics
NAME(S) OF RESEARCHER(S): Giovanni Bechelloni, Fabrizio de Benedetti, Giovanna Parisi
ORGANISATION: Centro di documentazione e di studi sull'informazione (CESDI)
ADDRESS: Via Fabio Massimo 60, 00192 Roma
DURATION OF PROJECT: Completed
SOURCE AND SCALE OF FINANCE: CNR Laboratorio per la ricerca e la documentazione; 4 million lire
RESEARCH METHODOLOGY: Postal questionnaire; interviews; conferences
LANGUAGE(S): Italian

377 TITLE OF PROJECT: Le fonti di informazione dell'economia italiana
DESCRIPTION: Examinations of sources (statistics and public documents) for the period 1945—66
NAME(S) OF RESEARCHER(S): Massimo Finoia (co-ordinator), Giuseppe Cosentino, Roberto Rosati and the team of the section 'Attività di formazione e ricerche regionali'
ORGANISATION: Associazione per lo sviluppo dell'industria nel Mezzogiorno (SVIMEZ)
ADDRESS: Via di Porta Pinciana 6, 00187 Roma
RESEARCH METHODOLOGY: Collection and critical analysis of documents
PUBLICATIONS: *Introduzione alle fonti di informazione dell'economia italiana*, Roneo-typed, Rome 1967, 87 pages
LANGUAGE(S): Italian

378 TITLE OF PROJECT: Rassegna della letteratura internazionale di
   irrea i modelli di previsione economica di lungo periodo e
   relativa valutazione critica
   DESCRIPTION: Critical review of literature of long-term economic
   planning
   NAME(S) OF RESEARCHER(S): Dott. Michelangelo Toglia,
   Dottoressa Rosanna Freschi
   ORGANISATION: Istituto nazionale per lo studio della
   congiuntura (ISCO)
   ADDRESS: Via Milano 20, Roma
   DURATION OF PROJECT: 1969–70
   SOURCE AND SCALE OF FINANCE: 3 million lire a year from the
   Ministero del bilancio e della programmazione economica
   PUBLICATIONS: Technical reports to the Ministero del bilancio
   e della programmazione economica
   LANGUAGE(S): Italian

United Kingdom/Royaume-Uni

379 TITLE OF PROJECT: Bristol Library of Commerce
   DESCRIPTION: Investigation of the Bristol Library of Commerce
   as an information service
   NAME(S) OF RESEARCHER(S): A.H. Thompson
   ORGANISATION: Bristol Public Libraries
   ADDRESS: College Green, Bristol
   DURATION OF PROJECT: Commenced in October 1969
   LANGUAGE(S): English

380 TITLE OF PROJECT: Critical evaluation of economics literature
   NAME(S) OF RESEARCHER(S): J. Fletcher (now at University of
   Warwick Library)
   ORGANISATION: Loughborough University of Technology, Library
   ADDRESS: Loughborough University of Technology, Loughborough,
   LE11 3TU
   RESEARCH METHODOLOGY: Citation analysis
   PUBLICATIONS: J. Fletcher, *The Use of Economics Literature*,
   Butterworths, 1971
   LANGUAGE(S): English

Education/Éducation

381 TITLE OF PROJECT: Bildungsforschungsdokumentation in
   Österreich
   DESCRIPTION: Description of Austrian research projects in the
   field of education research that have started since, or were
   planned after, September 1971
   NAME(S) OF RESEARCHER(S): Dr. Adamec
   ORGANISATION: Institut für Bildungs- und Entwicklungsforschung/
   Institute for Research in Education and Development
   ADDRESS: A-1010 Wien, Schottenbastei 6
   DURATION OF PROJECT: September 1971 — August 1972
   SOURCE OF FINANCE: BMfU (Ministry of Education)
   LANGUAGE(S): German

France

382 TITLE OF PROJECT: Groupe d'information documentaire
   DESCRIPTION: First phase: cataloguing of documents (photos, films,
   sound tapes) according to (1) the nature of the support, (2) the
   discipline concerned and (3) the level of use (fourth year class,
   fifth year class, etc.). Second phase: automatic documentary search
   NAME(S) OF RESEARCHER(S): C. Bonnefoi
   ORGANISATION: Institut pédagogique national
   ADDRESS: 29 rue d'Ulm, Paris 5^e
   DURATION OF PROJECT: First phase completed
   SOURCE OF FINANCE: Institut pédagogique national
   RESEARCH METHODOLOGY: Analysis of documents; elaboration
   of a very detailed thesaurus (it will have to take in 60,000 words)
   PUBLICATIONS: C. Bonnefoi *The Present State of the Pilot
   Experiment in Automatic Documentation,* Institut pédagogique
   national, Paris, November 1968. Article to appear in the next
   bulletin of the ADBS
   LANGUAGE(S): French

383 TITLE OF PROJECT: Projet de documentation pédagogique automatique
DESCRIPTION: First phase: study of automatic cataloguing of documents and setting up of a tele-cataloguing system joining the centres of Paris, Amiens and Toulouse. Second phase: automated document research, production of bibliographies
NAME(S) OF RESEARCHER(S): M. Majault, C. Petit (Directeur du CRDP de Toulouse), M. Arnal and M. Marie
ORGANISATION: Institut pédagogique national
ADDRESS: 3 rue Roquelaine, Toulouse 31
DURATION OF PROJECT: Completed
SOURCE OF FINANCE: Institut pédagogique national
RESEARCH METHODOLOGY: Development of a thesaurus
LANGUAGE(S): French

United Kingdom/Royaume-Uni

384 TITLE OF PROJECT: Library provision for adult education
DESCRIPTION: Survey of library provision for adult education agencies in North-East England
NAME(S) OF RESEARCHER(S): D.T. Lewis, K. O'Connor
ORGANISATION: Leeds Polytechnic, Department of Librarianship
ADDRESS: Calverley Street, Leeds LS1 3HE
DURATION OF PROJECT: Commenced in 1969
RESEARCH METHODOLOGY: Questionnaire

385 TITLE OF PROJECT: Problems of teachers in obtaining academic information
DESCRIPTION: Particularly related to curriculum development
NAME(S) OF RESEARCHER(S): F.A. Clements, G. Hammond
ORGANISATION: College of St Mark and St John
ADDRESS: Albert Road, Devonport, Plymouth
DURATION OF PROJECT: Commenced in 1969
SOURCE OF FINANCE: In house
LANGUAGE(S): English

386 TITLE OF PROJECT: Research and Development for Sociology of Education Abstracts
DESCRIPTION: The study will include presentation of alternative methods of information transfer

NAME(S) OF RESEARCHER(S): Research Fellow, 15 Norham Gardens, Oxford
ORGANISATION: Oxford University, Department of Education
DURATION OF PROJECT: October 1968 to October 1973
SOURCE OF FINANCE: UK Government Office for Scientific and Technical Information
RESEARCH METHODOLOGY: (1) Development of improved retrieval system likely to be of use in a wide area of the social sciences; (2) user study of abstracting journals' past and present performance, with comparison of possible future outputs and formats
LANGUAGE(S): English

Environmental Planning/ Planification de l'Environnement

Italy/Italie

387 TITLE OF PROJECT: UDC thesaurus
   DESCRIPTION: Multiple relationships between UDC terms
      relating to water and a keyword thesaurus on the subject
   NAME(S) OF RESEARCHER(S): Dott. Francesco Chiapetti
   ORGANISATION: Istituto di ricerca sulle acque del Consiglio
      Nazionale delle Ricerche
   ADDRESS: Via Reno 1, Roma
   DURATION OF PROJECT: Completed, but with possibility of
      further development work on computers
   SOURCE OF FINANCE: Consiglio Nazionale delle Ricerche
   LANGUAGE(S): Italian

United Kingdom/Royaume-Uni

388 TITLE OF PROJECT: Information needs for urban development in
      sub-regional planning
   DESCRIPTION: Exploration of information requirements of
      planners
   NAME(S) OF RESEARCHER(S): P. Hall
   ORGANISATION: University of Reading, Department of Geography
   ADDRESS: Whiteknights Park, Reading, Berks
   DURATION OF PROJECT: 1969–71
   LANGUAGE(S): English

389 TITLE OF PROJECT: Organisation of information for planning
   DESCRIPTION: (1) to investigate the scope of planning
      documentation (both published and unpublished), its composition,
      structure and availability, and to assemble a representative
      collection of such information. (2) To study the organisation of
      planning information for 'input' and 'output' respectively

167

NAME(S) OF RESEARCHER(S): Mrs B. White, under the
supervision of R.T. Bigwood
ORGANISATION: Planning Research Unit, Department of Urban
Design and Regional Planning, Edinburgh University
DURATION OF PROJECT: Three years, starting in 1971
SOURCE AND SCALE OF FINANCE: Office for Scientific and
Technical Information (£29,450)
RESEARCH METHODOLOGY: Study of resources by visiting
libraries and institutions
LANGUAGE(S): English

NOTE: See also entry 427

Ergonomics/Ergonomie

United Kingdom/Royaume-Uni

390 TITLE OF PROJECT: Ergonomics information
NAME(S) OF RESEARCHER(S): Professor N.A. Dudley,
J.B. Kidd
ORGANISATION: Birmingham University, Department of
Engineering Production
ADDRESS: Birmingham 15
DURATION OF PROJECT: 1968–71
SOURCE OF FINANCE: Office for Scientific and Technical
Information
LANGUAGE(S): English

Geography/Géographie

391 TITLE OF PROJECT: Computer techniques in indexing and
dissemination of geographical abstracts
NAME(S) OF RESEARCHER(S): Professor K.M. Clayton
ORGANISATION: University of East Anglia, School of
Environmental Sciences
ADDRESS: Earlham Hall, Norwich NOR 88C
LANGUAGE(S): English

History/Histoire

France

392 TITLE OF PROJECT: Statistique générale de la France

DESCRIPTION: Incorporated data: census returns and movements of population; agricultural inquiries; industrial inquiries; accounts of businesses, hospitals and prisons (relating to France in the 19th and 20th centuries)

ORGANISATION: Centre de Recherches historiques (CRH), Maison des Sciences de l'Homme

ADDRESS: 54 boulevard Raspail, 75 Paris 6^e

DURATION OF PROJECT: Completed June 1971

SOURCE OF FINANCE: Centre national de la Recherche scientifique; École pratique des hautes Études (Direction supérieure de l'Enseignement); University of Michigan

RESEARCH METHODOLOGY: Processing by IBM-OSIRIS II of the 150 volumes in the Bibliothèque nationale relating to the general statistics of France

PUBLICATIONS: A guide for users

LANGUAGE(S): English and French

Linguistics/Linguistique

France

393 TITLE OF PROJECT: Analyse automatique de texte
   DESCRIPTION: Production of a summary from key phrases;
      research into an automatic classification of concepts
   NAME(S) OF RESEARCHER(S): M. Deransart and C. Pointeau
   ORGANISATION: Institut de Recherche d'Informatique et
      d'Automatique (IRIA). Département de Documentation automatique
   ADDRESS: Domaine de Voluceau, 78 Rocquencourt
   SOURCE OF FINANCE: IRIA
   RESEARCH METHODOLOGY: Application of the methods of
      formal linguistics to the treatment of the résumés of the
      Documentation française. Inquiry made of users of the
      Documentation française
   LANGUAGE(S): French

394 TITLE OF PROJECT: Analyse lexicologique
   DESCRIPTION: Mechanisation of French linguistic bibliography
   NAME(S) OF RESEARCHER(S): B. Quemada
   ORGANISATION: Laboratoire d'Analyse lexicologique, Besançon
   ADDRESS: Faculté des Lettres et Sciences humaines, 25 Besançon
   SOURCE OF FINANCE: CNRS
   PUBLICATIONS: 'Essai de mécanisation de la bibliographie
      linguistique française' *Bulletin d'Information du Laboratoire
      d'Analyse lexicologqiue, VII,* pp. 17–51
   LANGUAGE(S): French

395 TITLE OF PROJECT: Analyse sémantique appliquée à la
      documentation
   DESCRIPTION: Establishment of a notional system; automatic
      translation of a résumé into a graph, the points of intersection
      of which are the descriptors and the lines of intersection one or
      other of the three relations of Syntol
   NAME(S) OF RESEARCHER(S): N. Bely, A. Borillo, J. Virbel,
      N. Siot-Decauville, J.C. Gardin

ORGANISATION: CNRS, Section d'Automatique documentaire et linguistique
ADDRESS: 31 chemin Joseph Aiguier, 13 Marseille 9^e
SOURCE OF FINANCE: CNRS
PUBLICATIONS: *Procédures d'Analyse sémantique appliquées à la Documentation scientifique*, Gauthiers Villars, 1970
LANGUAGE(S): French

396 TITLE OF PROJECT: Liste des descripteurs pour une documentation dans le domaine linguistique
NAME(S) OF RESEARCHER(S): A. Quincieux
ORGANISATION: Centre de Recherche et d'Applications linguistiques de Nancy
ADDRESS: CRAL, Faculté des Lettres et Sciences Humaines, 54 Nancy
PUBLICATIONS: 'Liste des descripteurs pour une documentation dans le domaine linguistique' *Publ. linguistiques de la Faculté des Lettres et Sciences humaines de Nancy* 8, Nancy 1969
LANGUAGE(S): French

397 TITLE OF PROJECT: Recherche en vue de la constitution d'un langage documentaire en linguistique
DESCRIPTION: This research has two aims: (1) constitution of a thesaurus (formed from descriptors) and (2) establishment of a suitable syntax for the codification of résumés
NAME(S) OF RESEARCHER(S): J. C. Anscombre, M.C. Barbault, H. du Chazaud, M. Lacoste
ORGANISATION: Centre de Documentation Sciences humaines du Centre national de la Recherche scientifique (CNRS)
ADDRESS: 54 boulevard Raspail, Paris 6^e
SOURCE OF FINANCE: CNRS
RESEARCH METHODOLOGY: Inquiry into the needs of users, and work on résumés
PUBLICATIONS: *Eléments de Recherche en vue de la Constitution d'un Langage documentaire*, Paris, n.d., CDSH–CNRS
LANGUAGE(S): French

398 TITLE OF PROJECT: Recherche pour un trésor de la langue française
DESCRIPTION: Preparation of a thesaurus of French linguistics

173

NAME(S) OF RESEARCHER(S): P. Imbs, E. Martin, E. Schneider,
A. Becker, H. Gerner, M. Jacquemin, F. Surdel
ORGANISATION: Centre de Recherche pour un Trésor de la
Langue française, CNRS
ADDRESS: 44 avenue de la Libération, 54 Nancy
SOURCE OF FINANCE: CNRS
LANGUAGE(S): French

399 TITLE OF PROJECT: Traduction automatique
DESCRIPTION: Model of automatic translation and study of
linguistic problems
NAME(S) OF RESEARCHER(S): C. Bourguignon, C. de Vigna,
M. Dupraz, N. Nedobejkine, H. Panchard, J.L. Riers, C. Fuchs,
R. Stiers, L. Torre, J. Rouault, G. Veillon, B. Vauquois
ORGANISATION: Centre d'Étude pour la Traduction automatique,
CNRS
ADDRESS: CETA, Cedex 53, 38 Grenoble Gare
SOURCE OF FINANCE: CNRS
RESEARCH METHODOLOGY: Method of formal linguistics
PUBLICATIONS: 'Modèles et algorithmes pour la traduction
automatique' (thesis by G. Veillon), *Documents CETA*, Faculté
des Sciences de Grenoble, 1970; B. Vauquois, 'Traduction
automatique des langues' *Traité de Pratique informatique*, 1970,
pp. 5–26; J. Rouault, 'Problèmes posés par la formation et
l'actualisation d'une lexis'; 'Contribution préliminaire à la
construction d'une grammaire de reconnaissance du français'
(thesis by C. Fuchs), Faculté des Lettres et Sciences humaines,
Paris 1971
LANGUAGE(S): French

400 TITLE OF PROJECT: Traitement automatique de textes
DESCRIPTION: Formalisation of interchangeable grammars;
application to automatic processing of documents and
documentation
NAME(S) OF RESEARCHER(S): M.C. Barbault and Q.P. Descles
ORGANISATION: Centre de Documentation Sciences humaines
du CNRS. Faculté des Sciences de Paris VII
ADDRESS: 54 boulevard Raspail, Paris 6^e
SOURCE OF FINANCE: CNRS

PUBLICATIONS: *Approches structurelle et catègorielle du Système de Transition avec Application à la Science du Calcul et à la Linguistique mathématique,* Faculté des Sciences, Paris 1970; 'Vers une formalisation des grammaires transformationelles' *Mathèmatiques et Sciences humaines* 34, 1971; 'Vers un traitement automatique des textes' *Revue de Linguistique Appliquée*, 1971
LANGUAGE(S): French

Management

Italy/Italie

401 TITLE OF PROJECT: La coordination des langages nationaux dans les services d'administration
DESCRIPTION: Research into problems of communication in the fields of management and administration
NAME(S) OF RESEARCHER(S): Roberto Artioli, Arnaldo Bagnases, Tina de Castro
ORGANISATION: Programma SEDOC
ADDRESS: Via Ventimiglia 115, 10126 Torino
DURATION OF PROJECT: Completed
SOURCE OF FINANCE: Consiglio Nazionale delle Ricerche
RESEARCH METHODOLOGY: Interviews, experimental observation, meetings
PUBLICATIONS: Proceedings of two meetings, entitled (1) 'La coordination des languages nationaux dans les sciences de l'administration' (2) 'Langage et communication dans l'entreprise moderne; quelques considérations pour un project de recherche'
LANGUAGE(S): Italian, French

United Kingdom/Royaume-Uni

402 TITLE OF PROJECT: Development of management documentation in Great Britain and Ireland
NAME(S) OF RESEARCHER(S): K.G.B. Bakewell (now at Liverpool Polytechnic)
ORGANISATION: Queen's University of Belfast
ADDRESS: 7 University Terrace, Belfast BT7 1NN
DURATION OF PROJECT: 1969—71
LANGUAGE(S): English

403 TITLE OF PROJECT: Faceted classification for business studies
NAME(S) OF RESEARCHER(S): A.F. Earle, K.D.C. Vernon
ORGANISATION: London Graduate School of Business Studies

ADDRESS: Sussex Place, Regents Park, London NW1 4SA
DURATION OF PROJECT: Commenced in 1967
SOURCE OF FINANCE: Office for Scientific and Technical
  Information
LANGUAGE(S): English

404 TITLE OF PROJECT: Information requirements of teachers and
  research workers in management studies
NAME(S) OF RESEARCHER(S): J.D. Dews
ORGANISATION: Manchester Business School, Library
ADDRESS: Booth Street West, Manchester M15 6PB
DURATION OF PROJECT: Completed
SOURCE OF FINANCE: Office for Scientific and Technical
  Information
RESEARCH METHODOLOGY: User study
PUBLICATIONS: J.D. Dews, *The Use of Information Sources by
  Teachers and Research Workers in the Field of Business Studies,*
  Report to OSTI, 1970
LANGUAGE(S): English

405 TITLE OF PROJECT: Investigation into the validity and value of
  post-coordinate indexing techniques within the fields of
  management and economic science
NAMES OF RESEARCHER(S): K.G.B. Bakewell, V. de P. Roper,
  E.J. Hunter
ORGANISATION: Liverpool Polytechnic, School of Librarianship
ADDRESS: Tithebarn Street, Liverpool 2
DURATION OF PROJECT: 1966–71
SOURCE OF FINANCE: In house
LANGUAGE(S): English

406 TITLE OF PROJECT: Subject indexing the literature of business
  management
DESCRIPTION: Use of BIM (British Institute of Management)
  management thesaurus; retrieval evaluations
NAME(S) OF RESEARCHER(S): J. Burkett
ORGANISATION: Ealing Technical College, School of Librarianship
ADDRESS: Ealing, London W5
DURATION OF PROJECT: Commenced in 1968
SOURCE OF FINANCE: Conducted jointly with the BIM
LANGUAGE(S): English

Political Science/
Sciences Politiques

France

407 TITLE OF PROJECT: Sociologie électorale
DESCRIPTION: (1) Individual references of candidates at French
elections; (2) election results (1870 to date)
NAME(S) OF RESEARCHER(S): Messrs Dupeux and Boudon
(directors of the project)
ORGANISATION: Centre de Recherches historiques (CRH),
Maison des Sciences de l'Homme
ADDRESS: 54 boulevard Raspail, 75 Paris 6^e
DURATION OF PROJECT: Completed in 1971
SOURCES OF FINANCE: Centre national de la Recherche
scientifique; Centre d'Études sociologiques; Fondation nationale
des Sciences politiques; Université de Bordeaux: University of
Michigan
RESEARCH METHODOLOGY: Processing by IBM of documents
from the Archives nationales and from the archives and library
of the Assemblée nationale
PUBLICATIONS: A guide for users
LANGUAGE(S): French principally

408 TITLE OF PROJECT: Préparation et expérimentation d'un
thésaurus pour le traitement de l'information en science politique
DESCRIPTION: Establishment of a structured bilingual
vocabulary (French–English) of terms required to describe the
contents of political science documents, and for research, through
classifying the information contained in these documents.
Experimental application to the preparation of some indexes and
bibliographies
NAME(S) OF RESEARCHER(S): Jean Meyriat (director of the
project)
ORGANISATION: Fondation nationale des Sciences politiques
ADDRESS: 27 rue Saint-Guillaume, 75 Paris 7^e
DURATION OF PROJECT: 1970–72

SOURCE OF FINANCE: Les Services de Documentation de la
Fondation nationale des Sciences politiques (no specified budget)
RESEARCH METHODOLOGY: Comparison of existing vocabularies
and lexicons, analysis of the indexes of specialist bibliographies,
analysis of primary documents
PUBLICATIONS: The thesaurus is destined for publication when
completed
LANGUAGE(S): English and French

Italy/Italie

409 TITLE OF PROJECT: Bibliografia generale italiana per le scienze
giuridice e politiche.
DESCRIPTION: Development of bibliographical data base for the
political and legal sciences
NAME(S) OF RESEARCHER(S): Sanfilippo, Abbondanze,
Napolitano, Firpo
ORGANISATION: Istituto per la documentazione giuridica del
Consiglio Nazionale delle Ricerche
ADDRESS: Via Panciatichi 56/16, 50127 Firenze
DURATION OF PROJECT: Commenced in 1970
SOURCE OF FINANCE: Consiglio Nazionale delle Ricerche
RESEARCH METHODOLOGY: Collection and analysis of the Italian
literature; input to machine-readable data base
LANGUAGE(S): Italian

Sweden/Suède

410 TITLE OF PROJECT: Juridical documentation
DESCRIPTION: Collecting and arranging material concerning
international legislation (especially conventions)
NAME(S) OF RESEARCHER(S): Professor Jan Hellner
ORGANISATION: University of Stockholm
ADDRESS: Box 6801, S113 86 Stockholm
DURATION OF PROJECT: Completed
SOURCE AND SCALE OF FINANCE: Application for a grant
of Skr. 28,000 from the Swedish Council for Scientific
Information and Documentation
LANGUAGE(S): Swedish

179

411 TITLE OF PROJECT: Guide to the political and secret department
records in the India Office Records, 1750–1947
NAME(S) OF RESEARCHER(S): Professor R. Irwin,
A.G. Watson, M.I. Moir
ORGANISATION: London University, University College School of
Library, Archive and Information Studies
ADDRESS: University College, Gower Street, London WC1
DURATION OF PROJECT: 1967–71
LANGUAGE(S): English

Psychology/Psychologie

412 TITLE OF PROJECT: Documentation of psychology
NAME(S) OF RESEARCHER(S): Professor T. Kempner,
  C.K. Elliott
ORGANISATION: Bradford University, Management Centre
ADDRESS: Bradford University, Great Harton Road, Bradford 7
DURATION OF PROJECT: Commenced in 1968
LANGUAGE(S): English

Social and Behavioural Sciences/ Sciences Sociales et Sciences du Comportement

Austria/Autriche

413 TITLE OF PROJECT: Forschungsdokumentation/Research in Austria
DESCRIPTION: Documentation of research institutions and organisations and of research projects
ORGANISATION: Bundesministerium für Wissenschaft und Forschung, Büro für Hochschulplanung
ADDRESS: A-1014 Wien, Minoritenplatz 5
RESEARCH METHODOLOGY: Data is taken from the Österreichisches Statistisches Zentralamt's biennial investigation of research and development in Austria
PUBLICATIONS: *Österreichischer Forschungsstättenkatalog*
LANGUAGE(S): German

Belgium/Belgique

414 TITLE OF PROJECT: Séminaire sur l'introduction de l'automatisation dans les sciences humaines, 1971
ORGANISATION: Association des Bibliothécaires et Archivistes de Belgique
ADDRESS: Boulevard de l'Empereur 4, 1000 Bruxelles

France

415 TITLE OF PROJECT: Direction des recherches sur la méthodologie
de l'information scientifique dans les sciences sociales
DESCRIPTION: Organisation and co-ordination of a series of
researches, generally taking the form of a treatise or doctoral
thesis, on the theoretical, methodological and practical problems
posed by the circulation and utilisation of scientific information
in the social sciences
NAME(S) OF RESEARCHER(S): Jean Meyriat, (director of studies)
and members of his Séminaire de l'École pratique des hautes
Études
ORGANISATION: École des hautes Études en Sciences sociales,
6ème section — Sciences économiques et sociales
ADDRESS: 54 rue de Varenne, 75 Paris 7^e
DURATION OF PROJECT: No limit
SOURCE AND SCALE OF FINANCE: Services given free
RESEARCH METHODOLOGY: Varies according to the cases
studied. Inquiries by questionnaire and interview, statistical
analyses of documents, analyses of contents, citation studies, etc.
PUBLICATIONS: Certain of these works will be published, in the
form either of articles or of monographs
LANGUAGE(S): French

International

416 TITLE OF PROJECT: Social science documentation and information
services
DESCRIPTION: Drawing up of a data storage and retrieval system
for banking social science data needed by UNESCO in pursuing its
programme projects
NAME(S) OF RESEARCHER(S): A. Glinkine (Director, IDSS, officer
responsible for the project); Ester M. Ronquillo (Centre Programme
Specialist, Project Officer)
ORGANISATION: UNESCO, Social Science Documentation Centre
ADDRESS: Place de Fontenoy, 75 Paris 7^e, France
DURATION OF PROJECT: 1969—72
SOURCE AND SCALE OF FINANCE: Financed by UNESCO
under the Regular Programme 1971; $21,000, salaries of officers
and staff excluded

RESEARCH METHODOLOGY: Letter-circular plus questionnaire; information search by scanning the literature; correspondence; direct information obtained by specialists
PUBLICATIONS: Inventories, bibliographies, surveys
LANGUAGE(S): English and French

Italy/Italie

417 TITLE OF PROJECT: Raccolta e elaborazione dei dati in materia economica e sociale
DESCRIPTION: Collection and elaboration of statistical data in economic and social subjects; constitution of two working groups; editing of reports, conferences
NAME(S) OF RESEARCHER(S): Several experts
ORGANISATION: (COSPOS) Comitato per le scienze politiche e sociali
ADDRESS: Viale Mazzini 88, 00195 Roma
DURATION OF PROJECT: Completed
RESEARCH METHODOLOGY: Collection of documentation, and meetings with experts
PUBLICATIONS: Roneo-typed reports. One of these reports, 'Limiti e carenze delle statistiche sull'istruzione', appeared in *Quindicinale di note e commenti*, 121, 15 June 1970, pp. 559–69. Information about the working group on social statistics was published in *Scienze sociali*, July 1970, pp.115–18
LANGUAGE(S): Italian

United Kingdom/Royaume-Uni

418 TITLE OF PROJECT: Acquisition and maintenance, on microfilm, of selected South Asian newspapers
NAME(S) OF RESEARCHER(S): B.H. Farmer, A.J.N. Richards, T.M. Thatcher
ORGANISATION: Cambridge University, Centre for South Asian Studies
ADDRESS: Cambridge CB2 1TT
LANGUAGE(S): Various

184

419 TITLE OF PROJECT: Collection and maintenance of an archive of mainly unpublished material on South Asia
NAME(S) OF RESEARCHER(S): B.H. Farmer
ORGANISATION: Cambridge University, Centre for South Asian Studies
ADDRESS: Cambridge CB2 1TT
DURATION OF PROJECT: Commenced in 1967
LANGUAGE(S): Various

420 TITLE OF PROJECT: Combined bibliographical project on African literature
DESCRIPTION: Production of bibliographical data on the social science literature of sub-Saharan Africa, for input into the automatic retrieval system of the Centre d'Études africaines — CARDAN — in Paris
ORGANISATION: University of Cambridge, African Studies Centre
ADDRESS: Sidgwick Avenue, Cambridge
DURATION OF PROJECT: Continuing
SOURCE OF FINANCE: Grant from Leverhulme Trust
RESEARCH METHODOLOGY: Monitoring the literature; supply of data to CARDAN for dissemination to users

421 TITLE OF PROJECT: Co-operation in the storage, retrieval and dissemination of social science data in the fields of politics, economics and commerce within Western Europe
NAME(S) OF RESEARCHER(S): R. Pryce, M. Guha
ORGANISATION: Sussex University, Centre for Contemporary European Studies
ADDRESS: Falmer, Brighton BN1 9QH

422 TITLE OF PROJECT: Design of Information Systems in the Social Sciences (DISISS)
DESCRIPTION: (1) Bibliometric studies of the structure of the primary literature and its coverage by secondary services; citation studies, etc. (2) Experimental services to test hypotheses concerning types and forms of information service aimed at different categories of user, with appropriate evaluation. (3) Modelling of information system with a view to optimisation; with the aid of a conceptual macro-model, detailed micro-models will be constructed of elements such as abstracting tools

NAME(S) OF RESEARCHER(S): Project head – M.B. Line;
Researchers – J.M. Brittain, S.A. Roberts, Miss B. Skelton,
R.G. Bradshaw, P. Burridge
ORGANISATION: University of Bath
ADDRESS: University Library, Claverton Down, Bath BA2 7AY
DURATION OF PROJECT: From January 1971 – March 1975
SOURCE OF FINANCE: Office for Scientific and Technical
Information
RESEARCH METHODOLOGY: See above
LANGUAGE(S): English

423 TITLE OF PROJECT: Development of computerised London
register of research and information – ACOMPLIS (A
Computerised London Information Service)
DESCRIPTION: Using the IBM Document Processing System to
provide a comprehensive register relevant to local government in
London
NAME(S) OF RESEARCHER(S): C.A.F. Russell, A.T. Gore,
A.A. Peacock, G. Berlin
ORGANISATION: Greater London Council, Intelligence Unit
ADDRESS: County Hall, London SE1
DURATION OF PROJECT: Commenced in 1968
LANGUAGE(S): English

424 TITLE OF PROJECT: Experimental information service in the
social sciences
DESCRIPTION: Development of SDI services to social science
researchers; evaluation of services
NAME(S) OF RESEARCHER(S): M.B. Line (project head),
D. Cunningham, S. Evans
ORGANISATION: University of Bath
ADDRESS: University Library, Claverton Down, Bath BA2 7AY
DURATION OF PROJECT: 1968–71
SOURCE OF FINANCE: Office for Scientific and
Technical Information
PUBLICATIONS: *Report on Work Carried out in 1969,* Bath
University of Technology, 1970; *Report on Work Carried out in
1970*, Bath University of Technology, 1971
LANGUAGE(S): English

425 TITLE OF PROJECT: Flow of information in local government
NAME(S) OF RESEARCHER(S): D.E. Davinson, D. Daintree
ORGANISATION: Leeds Polytechnic, Department of
Librarianship and Information Science
ADDRESS: Calverley Street, Leeds LS1 7RH
DURATION OF PROJECT: 1968–71
LANGUAGE(S): English

426 TITLE OF PROJECT: Guide to government data
DESCRIPTION: Comprehensive guide to published and
unpublished data
NAME(S) OF RESEARCHER(S): A.F. Comfort
ORGANISATION: British Library of Political and Economic
Science
ADDRESS: Houghton Street, London WC2
DURATION OF PROJECT: 1969–71
LANGUAGE(S): English

427 TITLE OF PROJECT: Information for planning
DESCRIPTION: Exchange of information between practitioners in
local authorities
NAME(S) OF RESEARCHER(S): Mrs B. White
ORGANISATION: The Planning Exchange
ADDRESS: 186 Bath Street, Glasgow G2 4HG
DURATION OF PROJECT: Continuing
RESEARCH METHODOLOGY: Following up work carried out on
the organisation of information for planning project (see
entry 389)
PUBLICATIONS: B. White, *Sourcebook of Information for
Planning*, London, Bingley 1971; B. White, *Information for
Planning . . .: Report of Studies,* OSTI Report no. 5198,
Edinburgh University (Planning Research Unit, Edinburgh 1974;
B. White, *The Literature and Study of Urban and Regional
Planning,* London, Bingley 1974
LANGUAGE(S): English

428 TITLE OF PROJECT: Regional statistics
DESCRIPTION: Aimed at providing a better series of British regional
statistics for major economic and social variables, both by making
existing series more compatible and by introducing selected new,
and hitherto unavailable series

NAME(S) OF RESEARCHER(S): Professor J.P. Lewis,
Lady Bowden
ORGANISATION: Manchester University, Centre for Urban and
Regional Research
ADDRESS: Oxford Road, Manchester M13 9PL
DURATION OF PROJECT: 1968–70
SOURCE OF FINANCE: Social Science Research Council
LANGUAGE(S): English

429 TITLE OF PROJECT: Social Science Research Council Data Bank
DESCRIPTION: Storage of machine-readable data relating to
social and economic affairs and deriving from academic,
commercial and government sources, so as to make the data
available for further analysis
NAME(S) OF RESEARCHER(S): D.J.G. Farlie, T.E. Roughley
ORGANISATION: Essex University, SSRC Data Bank
ADDRESS: Wivenhoe Park, Colchester, Essex
DURATION OF PROJECT: 1967–72
SOURCE OF FINANCE: SSRC
LANGUAGE(S): English

Social Policy and
Social Administration/
Politique Sociale et
Administration Sociale

France

430 TITLE OF PROJECT: Modalités d'une 'Banque de Données sur la
Formation permanente'
DESCRIPTION: Collecting and automated exploitation of data on
further education (information about adult education,
administration, ministries involved, and specialist agencies)
NAME(S) OF RESEARCHER(S): M. Lesne, J.M. Thiveaud,
P.L. Eche, M. Fiskus (technical adviser, information side)
ORGANISATION: Institut national pour la Formation des Adultes
ADDRESS: 18 rue des Tilleuls, 92 Boulogne
DURATION OF PROJECT: Completed
SOURCE OF FINANCE: Ministère de l'Éducation nationale,
Direction de la Formation continué (M. Vatier)
RESEARCH METHODOLOGY: Inquiries of training organisations,
professional organisations, enterprises; automatic processing of
the data by the SINBAD (Système informatique pour Banque de
Données) information system
LANGUAGE(S): French

International

431 TITLE OF PROJECT: Centre international de Documentation en
Loisir (CIDOL)
DESCRIPTION: Planning of a network of documentation centres on
leisure and culture, to be connected at one central source (in
Montreal); processing and dissemination of the scientific
documentation on the subject; development of a thesaurus for
information retrieval

189

ORGANISATION: Comité de Recherche du Loisir et de la Culture
populaire de l'Association Internationale de Sociologie.
Président – J. Dumazedier (Paris CNRS); Secrétaire général –
M. Laplante (Université du Québec, Montreal)
ADDRESS: Centre d'Études sociologiques, 82 rue Cardinet, Paris
17e, France; Secrétariat du Comité de Recherche du Loisir,
420 Ouest rue Lagauchetière, Ch. 425, Montreal 128e, PQ, Canada
DURATION OF PROJECT: Operative phase finished in 1972.
Continuing
SOURCES OF FINANCE: Various. Grants and contracts in various
interested countries; co-operation with the Association
Internationale de Sociologie (AIS)
RESEARCH METHODOLOGY: Compilation of a specialised
bilingual thesaurus. Coordinate index and processing by
computer (CDC 6400)
PUBLICATIONS: Regular periodical in the form of current
bibliographies and review with abstracts; multilingual bibliography
on the sociology of leisure (1945–65) published in *Current
Sociology*, 1968

United Kingdom/Royaume-Uni

432 TITLE OF PROJECT: Compilation of classification and thesaurus
in the health sciences for nursing libraries
NAME(S) OF RESEARCHER(S): Mrs S. Cook
ORGANISATION: Polytechnic of North London, School of
Librarianship
ADDRESS: 207–25 Essex Road, London N1
SOURCE OF FINANCE: Library Association
LANGUAGE(S): English

433 TITLE OF PROJECT: Future needs in writing and reading aids for
the disabled
NAME(S) OF RESEARCHER(S): A. Shaw
ORGANISATION: The Library Association
ADDRESS: 7 Ridgmount Street, London WC1E 7AE
DURATION OF PROJECT: Commenced in 1968
SOURCE OF FINANCE: Library Association
LANGUAGE(S): English

434 TITLE OF PROJECT: United Kingdom National Documentation
Centre for Sport, Physical Education and Recreation
DESCRIPTION: Planning and operation of a documentation and
information service
NAME(S) OF RESEARCHER(S): G.A. Bell
ORGANISATION: University of Birmingham
ADDRESS: PO Box 363, Birmingham B15 2TT (Telephone
021-472-7410)
DURATION OF PROJECT: Continuing
SOURCE OF FINANCE: Department of Education and Science:
Sports Council
LANGUAGE(S): English

435 TITLE OF PROJECT: Social work indexing
DESCRIPTION: Production of indexing language; comparisons
with other indexing systems
NAME(S) OF RESEARCHER(S): T.D. Wilson (now lecturer at the
University of Sheffield Postgraduate School of Librarianship
and Information Science), I.S. Simpson
ORGANISATION: School of Librarianship, Newcastle-upon-Tyne
Polytechnic
ADDRESS: Department of Librarianship, Faculty of Community and
Social Studies, Newcastle-upon-Tyne Polytechnic, Northumberland
Buildings, St. Mary's Place, Newcastle-upon-Tyne NE1 8ST
DURATION OF PROJECT: 1970
SOURCE OF FINANCE: Office for Scientific and Technical
Information
LANGUAGE(S): English

Sociology/Sociologie

Austria/Autriche

436 TITLE OF PROJECT: Regional-soziologische Dokumentation
DESCRIPTION: Documentation of effects on regional entities such
as districts, countries, etc., of any measures of sociological
relevance
NAME(S) OF RESEARCHER(S): Prof. Dr Kurt Freisitzer
ORGANISATION: Universität Graz, Institut für Soziologie
ADDRESS: A-5010 Graz, Universitätsstrasse 27/1
RESEARCH METHODOLOGY: Data is taken from official
statistics

Italy/Italie

437 TITLE OF PROJECT: Le ponti nel settore dell'organizzazione della
cultura e delle comunicazioni di massa
DESCRIPTION: Inventory of statistical sources, and examination of
methods of collecting and elaborating in the different sectors;
evaluation of the existing situation in the perspective of a policy
of cultural development
NAME(S) OF RESEARCHER(S): Giovanni Bechelloni
(co-ordinator), Bruno Amoroso, Giovanna Parisi, Piero Castello
ORGANISATION: Centro di documentazione e di studi
sull'informazione (CESDI)
ADDRESS: Via Fabio Massimo 60, 00192 Roma
DURATION OF PROJECT: Completed
SOURCE AND SCALE OF FINANCE: Istituto per la
programmazione economica (ISPE); 3 million lire
RESEARCH METHODOLOGY: Collection and critical analysis
of documents
PUBLICATIONS: The first part of the report has been published
in a Roneo-typed dossier, *Offerta e consumo di beni culturali*,
May 1971
LANGUAGE(S): Italian

438 TITLE OF PROJECT: Ricerca nell'ambito dell'automatic
  indexing di testi giuridici
  DESCRIPTION: Research into automated indexing of legal texts
  NAME(S) OF RESEARCHER(S): Angelo Gallizia (Director of
  project)
  ORGANISATION: Centro di documentazione automatica
  ADDRESS: Via Cuzani 10, Milano
  DURATION OF PROJECT: 1969–70
  SOURCE AND SCALE OF FINANCE: 8·4 million lire from CNR,
  Laboratorio di studi sulla ricerca e sulla documentazione
  RESEARCH METHODOLOGY: Computer-based experiments
  PUBLICATIONS: Research report
  LANGUAGE(S): Italian

Netherlands/Pays-Bas

439 TITLE OF PROJECT: Inquiry into the use of literature by social
  scientists
  DESCRIPTION: Inquiry into users' habits (response 50–60 per cent)
  NAME(S) OF RESEARCHER(S): Mrs. drs. H.P. Hogeweg de Haart;
  Drs. G.J.A. Riesthuis
  ORGANISATION: (1) Sociaal-wetenschappelijke Informatie- en
  Documentatiecentrum; (2) Sociologisch Instituut van de
  Rijksuniversiteit Utrecht
  ADDRESS: (1) Keizersgracht 569–571, Amsterdam; (2)
  Heidelberglaan 2, Utrecht
  DURATION OF PROJECT: Commenced in December 1969
  RESEARCH METHODOLOGY: Inquiry by mail
  LANGUAGE(S): Dutch

440 TITLE OF PROJECT: Research into sociological documentation
  in the Netherlands
  DESCRIPTION: To investigate (1) whether there are some aspects
  of sociological literature that are not documented at all; (2)
  whether any documentation centres offer anything that has
  already been done elsewhere; (3) qualitative aspects of these
  documentation centres
  NAME(S) OF RESEARCHER(S): Drs. G.J.A. Riesthuis
  ORGANISATION: Sociologisch Instituut van de Rijksuniversiteit
  Utrecht

193

ADDRESS: Heidelberglaan 2, Utrecht
DURATION OF PROJECT: About two years from late 1969
SOURCE AND SCALE OF FINANCE: Ministry of Education and
  Science; more than Hfl. 100,000
RESEARCH METHODOLOGY: Questionnaire
PUBLICATIONS: Report
LANGUAGE(S): Dutch

United Kingdom/Royaume-Uni

441 TITLE OF PROJECT: Use and flow of information in university
  research
DESCRIPTION: Examination of processes of scientific commun-
  ication in a university research environment in the field of
  nuclear physics; tests of research methodology
NAME(S) OF RESEARCHER(S): R.D. Whitley and A. McAlpine
ORGANISATION: Manchester Business School
ADDRESS: Booth Street West, Manchester M15 6PB
DURATION OF PROJECT: 1972–74
SOURCE OF FINANCE: UK Government, Office for Scientific and
  Technical Information
RESEARCH METHODOLOGY: Studies modelled on investigations
  (carried out by T.J. Allen of Massachusetts Institute of Technology)
  of information flow in industrial R & D units
LANGUAGE(S): English

Statistics/Statistiques

Austria/Autriche

442 TITLE OF PROJECT: ISIS (Intergriertes statistisches
Informationssystem)
DESCRIPTION: Computer-aided system of multi-dimensional
searching in statistical files
ORGANISATION: Österreichisches statistisches Zentralamt
ADDRESS: A-1010 Wien, Neue Burg
DURATION OF PROJECT: Continuing

Appendices/
Annexes

Appendix A

The following definitions were used in the 'Guide for Rapporteurs'.

1 *Information services* may have all or some of the following character-istics:

(a) They are organisations that provide services on request. A client takes the initiative by contacting the organisation and requesting some service (for example, a literature search, data processing), and the organisation will provide specific answers to the questions posed by the client.

(b) The material provided in response to the client's question is usually made available to him and becomes his property; it is often very specific, and not available in this form in any published works held in libraries, etc.

(c) Requests for the services provided by the organisations will be on an irregular basis (although some services, such as lists of new titles, may be provided regularly to members of the organisation).

In summary, the main feature of this category is that a client requests an organisation for information, which is passed back to him.

Rapporteurs should note that we do *not* wish to include libraries, unless they are specialised libraries providing a service that is not generally available elsewhere. Referral centres and clearing-houses should be included.

2 *Information sources* may have all or some of the following character-istics:

(a) They take the form of written material, usually published in some formal, permanent manner (for example, as an abstracting journal or indexing journal).

(b) They are generally available in places and from organisations other than those in which and for whom they are produced (for example, in libraries), or personal copies may be purchased. They may be distributed free, but more often only to those paying a subscription.

(c) Individuals use the material themselves. In this sense the source, once produced, is seen as passive, and the user as active.

(d)   Publication of the source is usually on a regular basis.

In summary, the main feature of this category is that the individual seeks out the source, and uses it himself to find the information he requires, without asking the producers of the source for a service or assistance.

3   *Information research.* Research projects dealing with information in the social sciences and for social scientists.

Annexe A

Les définitions suivantes ont été données dans le «Guide à l'intention des Rapporteurs»:

1 Les *services d'information* peuvent présenter la totalité ou quelques-unes seulement des caractéristiques suivantes:

(a) Ce sont des organisations qui fournissent des services sur demande. Un client prend l'initiative en se mettant en rapport avec l'organisation et en lui demandant certains services (par exemple, recherche biblio-graphique, traitement de données), et celle-ci fournit des réponses précises aux questions posées.

(b) Lorsque la documentation est fournie au client, elle devient en général sa propriété; elle est souvent très spécialisée et n'est disponible dans aucun des ouvrages publiés détenus par les bibliothèques, etc.

(c) Les demandes de services sont présentées aux organisations à intervalles irréguliers (bien que certains services puissent être fournis régulièrement aux membres de l'organisation, par exemple les listes de titres nouveaux).

En résumé, la principale caractéristique de ces services est qu'ils donnent des réponses aux demandes d'information formulées par leurs clients.

Les rapporteurs voudront bien noter que *nous ne désirons pas inclure* dans l'inventaire les noms des bibliothèques, à moins qu'elles ne soient spécialisées et fournissent un service que l'on ne peut obtenir ailleurs. En revanche, les centres de références et les centres d'échange devraient être inclus dans l'inventaire.

2 Les *sources d'information* peuvent présenter la totalité ou quelques-unes seulement des caractéristiques suivantes:

(a) Elles se présentent sous la forme de documentation écrite, géné-ralement publiée sous une forme définitive et officielle (par exemple résumés, index).

(b) Elles sont généralement disponibles dans des lieux et organisations autres que ceux dont elles émanent (par exemple dans des bibliothèques); ou alors on peut se les procurer à titre individuel. Elles sont parfois distribuées à titre gratuit, mais le plus souvent uniquement aux souscripteurs.

(c) Les détenteurs de la documentation l'utilisent eux-mêmes. Dans ce sens, la source, une fois établie, joue un rôle passif et l'utilisateur un rôle actif.

(d) La source est en général publiée périodiquement.

En résumé, la principale caractéristique de cette catégorie est qu'une personne se procure la source et l'utilise elle-même pour trouver les informations dont elle a besoin sans demander à l'organisation productrice un service ou une aide.

3 *La recherche en matière d'information.* Projets de recherche traitant de l'information dans les sciences sociales et pour les spécialistes en sciences sociales.

Appendix B/Annexe B

BIBLIOGRAPHICAL SOURCES LISTING INFORMATION AND DOCUMENTATION SERVICES

Austria/Autriche

Dokumentation und Information in Österreich, second edition Verlag Br. Hollinek, Vienna 1970, 100 pages. Prepared by the Österreichische Gesellschaft für Dokumentation und Bibliographie. Lists documentation and information centres in the social sciences, etc.

Belgium/Belgique

Centre national de Documentation scientifique et technique, *Inventaire des Centres belges de Recherches disposant d'une Bibliothèque ou d'un Service de Documentation,* second edition (edited by J. Verougstraete), Bibliothèque royale Albert 1er, Bruxelles 1971.

Canada

Special Libraries and Information Centres in Canada: a Directory (compiled by B.L. Anderson), Canadian Library Association, Ottawa 1970, 168 pages. Directory of 1075 units, including those in industry, business, government, research and higher education, and also various associations.

Europe

Directory of European Associations Part 1, 'National, industrial, trade and professional associations' (edited by I.G. Anderson), CBD Research Ltd. Beckenham 1971.

Finland/Finlande

Suomen Tieteellisteen Kirjastojen Opas (Guide to the research and special libraries of Finland (compiled by M. Liinamaa), fourth edition, Tieteellisten Kirjastojen Lautakunta, Helsinki 1971. Lists 397 libraries, stating their names and addresses, and providing information on their services, holdings, and the fields covered, etc.

France

Centre français de Documentation scientifique et technique, Association nationale de la Recherche technique, Paris 1971.

'Directory of documentation centres in France' in *Coopération technique* 33−4, 1963, pp.1−76.

Répertoire des Bibliothèques d'Études et Organismes de Documentation, Bibliothèque nationale, Paris 1971. Provides data on 3,200 libraries and documentation centres; subject index.

Germany/République fédérale d'Allemagne

Verzeichnis der Spezialbibliotheken in der Bundesrepublik Deutschland einschliesslich West Berlin (compiled by F. Meyen), F. Vieweg und Sohn, Brunswick 1970.

Verzeichnis von Schrifttum-Auskunftstellen (List of documentation centres), Beuth Vertrieb, Berlin 1962. Lists documentation centres in the social sciences, etc.

International

World Index of Social Science Institutions: Research, Advanced Training, Documentation and Professional Bodies − a special service of the International Social Science Journal, UNESCO, Paris 1970.

Ireland (Eire)/Irlande

Scientific and Technical Information in Ireland: a Review. National Science Council, Dublin 1972.

Italy/Italie

Guida delle biblioteche scientifiche e techniche e dei centri di document-azione Italiana, Consiglio Nazionale delle Ricerche, Rome 1965. Lists approx. 1,500 documentation centres.

Netherlands/Pays-Bas

Koninklijke Nederlandse Akademie van Wetenschappen, Sociaal-Wetenschappelijke Raad, Sociaal-wetenschappelijke Informatie- en Documentatiecentrum, *Wegwijzer: Maatschappijwetenschappen Biblio-theken en Documentatieinstellingen,* NV Noord-Hollandsche Uitgevers Maatschappij, Amsterdam 1971.

Switzerland/Suisse

Archive, Bibliotheken und Dokumentationsstellen der Schweiz, Schweiz-erische Vereinigung für Dokumentation, Berne 1958.

United Kingdom/Royaume-Uni

Aslib Directory vol. 2, 'Information sources in medicine, social sciences and the humanities' (edited by B.J. Wilson), Aslib, London 1970.

Directory of British Associations, third edition, 1971–72 (edited by G.P. Henderson and S.P.A. Henderson) CBD Research, Beckenham 1970.

Appendix C/Annexe C

Table 1

Summary of information services by country and subject

	Austria	Belgium	Canada	Finland	France	Germany (Federal Republic)	International	Ireland (Eire)	Italy	Japan	Netherlands	Norway	Sweden	Switzerland	United Kingdom
Anthropology					7										
Criminology		3			2		1		1		1				1
Demography			1												2
Economics		18	1	2	7	1	1		8	3	1				10
Education		5	6	1	4	3	4				2		1	2	17
Environmental planning	1	2	2	1	2	1	2		2					1	3
Ergonomics															1
Futurology							1								
Geography	1				1	1									
History				1	2		1								1
Linguistics															1
Management	2					1	1	1	5		1		1	2	1
Political science		3	1	1	2	2	7	1	4		2	1			6
Psychology		2		1	1				1						1
Social and behavioural sciences	1	11	5	1	7	4	3	1	1		4	1	1	2	12
Social policy and social administration		8	1		5	1	2								9
Sociology		3			1	3			2		1				1
Statistics		2	1	1			1		1			1			1

Table 2

Summary of information services by subject

Subject	No.
Social and behavioural sciences	54
Economics	52
Education	45
Political science	30
Social policy and social administration	26
Environmental planning	17
Management	15
Sociology	11
Criminology	9
Statistics	8
Anthropology	7
Psychology	6
History	5
Geography	3
Demography	3
Linguistics	1
Futurology	1
Ergonomics	1
Total	294

Table 3

Summary of information services by country

Country	No.
United Kingdom	67
Belgium	57
France	41
Italy	25
International	24
Canada	18
Germany (Federal Republic)	17
Netherlands	12
Finland	9
Switzerland	7
Austria	5
Sweden	4
Ireland (Eire)	3
Japan	3
Norway	2
Total	294

Index

General Index/Index général

220

224

228

Subject Index/Index par Sujets

Anthropology/Anthropologie

1–7, 209, 223, 236, 250, 321, 322

Area studies/Études régionales

2–4, 18, 37, 41, 44, 71, 74, 107, 137, 140, 141, 161, 166, 172, 173, 185, 186, 190, 201–3, 208, 215, 216, 218, 222, 224, 229, 236, 239, 240, 242, 243, 245, 246, 248, 249, 322, 323, 324, 338, 347, 348, 418–21

Criminology/Criminologie

8–16, 84, 259, 370, 409, 410

Demography/Démographie

17–19, 42, 209, 221, 262, 296, 297

Development/Développement

47, 49, 50, 52, 96, 103, 107, 183, 200, 203, 221, 224, 225, 228, 232, 250, 335, 364, 377

Documentation

230, 241, 300–4, 334, 337, 339, 340, 351–5, 357, 414, 416, 422, 427, 435, 439

Economics/Économie

20, 71, 118, 124, 146, 148, 170, 172, 197, 202, 203, 205, 212, 221, 223, 225, 226, 231, 232, 236, 238, 250, 288, 289, 298–300, 314, 319, 321, 327, 342, 358, 371–80

Education/Éducation

72–117, 197, 223, 225, 226, 231, 263, 301–8, 327, 381–6

235

Environmental Planning/Planification de l'Environnement

17, 57, 70, 90, 118–34, 210, 214, 231, 256, 283, 309–12, 358, 387–9, 423

Ergonomics/Ergonomie

135, 147, 390

Futurology/Futurologie

136

Geography/Géographie

56, 124, 137–9, 203, 221, 313, 321, 391

History/Histoire

3, 4, 7, 140–44, 172, 203, 221, 236, 238, 321, 392

International Affairs/Politiques internationales

178, 184, 189, 238, 248

Law/Droit

16, 29, 39, 120, 124, 169, 170, 171, 179, 180, 202, 212, 283, 365, 368, 409, 410, 438

Leisure/Loisir

115, 264, 279, 307, 361, 362, 431, 434

Linguistics/Linguistique

72, 81, 88, 103, 105, 106, 109, 145, 221, 301, 393–400

Management

22, 28, 30, 31, 38, 40, 42, 53, 60, 61, 64–7, 102, 146–60, 187, 196, 314, 315, 401–6

Marketing

25, 26, 61, 149

Media and Communication/Média et Communication

198, 204, 280, 281, 284, 286, 363, 366, 369, 437

Political Science/Sciences politiques

16, 161−90, 197, 202, 205, 207, 209, 210, 212, 214, 217, 223, 231, 236, 238, 248, 250, 299, 316, 317, 324, 327, 342, 407−11, 425, 426

Psychology/Psychologie

10, 97, 113, 191−6, 318, 327, 412

Public Administration/Administration publique

163, 174, 175, 177, 182, 187, 188, 197, 207, 212, 425

Social and Behavioural Sciences/Sciences sociales et Sciences du Comportement

66, 82, 197−250, 319−57, 364, 413−29

Social Policy and Social Administration/Politique Sociale et Administration Sociale

15, 41, 87, 177, 212, 251−76, 282, 287, 304, 344, 358−62, 430−5

Sociology/Sociologie

22, 42, 54, 63, 67, 72, 124, 167, 195, 203, 205, 209, 210, 213, 221, 223, 225, 226, 232, 250, 260, 277−87, 299, 304, 321, 363−9, 436−41

Statistics/Statistiques

28, 38, 55, 56, 69, 149, 173, 213, 234, 235, 281, 288−95, 370, 371, 417, 428, 429, 437, 442

Transport

57, 121, 129, 132

Country Index/Index par Pays

238

Italy/Italie

14, 50–7, 129, 130, 151–5, 178–81, 230, 284, 285, 293, 298–300, 305, 311, 315, 317, 342–5, 368, 369, 375–8, 387, 401, 409, 417, 437, 438

Japan/Japon

58–60

Netherlands/Pays-Bas

15, 61, 95, 96, 156, 182, 183, 231–4, 286, 306, 312, 346–51, 439, 440

Norway/Norvège

235, 294

Sweden/Suède

97, 157, 184, 236, 410

Switzerland/Suisse

98, 99, 131, 158, 159, 237, 238

United Kingdom/Royaume-Uni

16, 18, 19, 62–71, 100–17, 132–5, 144, 145, 160, 185–90, 196, 239–50, 268–76, 287, 295, 307, 308, 352–7, 379, 380, 384–6, 388–91, 402–6, 411, 412, 418–29, 432–5, 441

DATE DUE	
OCT 0 1 1990	